Yourcenar

Yourcenar

George Rousseau

HAUS PUBLISHING · LONDON

This English translation first published in Great Britain
in 2004 by Haus Publishing Limited
26 Cadogan Court
Draycott Avenue
London
SW3 3BX

Copyright © George Rousseau, 2004

The moral rights of the author have been asserted.

A CIP catalogue record for this book is available from the British Library

ISBN 1-904341-28-4

Typeset by Lobster Design

Printed and bound by Graphicom in Vicenza, Italy

Jacket images: Lebrecht/Rue des Archives

CONDITIONS OF SALE
All rights reserved. No part of this publication may be reproduced, stored in a retrieval system, or transmitted in any form or by any means, electronic, mechanical, photocopying, recording or otherwise, without the prior permission of the publisher.

This book is sold subject to the condition that it shall not, by way of trade or otherwise, be lent, re-sold, hired out or otherwise circulated without the publisher's prior consent in any form of binding or cover other than that in which it is published and without a similar condition including this condition being imposed on the subsequent purchaser

Contents

A Life of Contradictions	1
Passionate Classicist 1903–1929	21
Seductress and Traveller 1929–1939	36
America, America 1940–1951	49
Yourcenar as Hadrian 1951–1955	59
Yourcenar as Zeno 1955–1979	79
Immortal Exile: 1979–1987	99
Epilogue: Is Yourcenar a Gay Writer?	118
Notes	*128*
Chronology	*132*
Works by Marguerite Yourcenar	*140*
Further Reading	*146*
Picture Sources	*148*
A Note on the Author	*148*
Index	*149*

A Life of Contradictions

Why does the writing make us chase the writer?
Why can't we leave well enough alone?
                    Julian Barnes, *Flaubert's Parrot*[1]

The sad truth about Marguerite Yourcenar is that many readers will need to ask who she was. In France her name is still a household word but not in the Anglo-American world: in Britain her former bestsellers are almost all out of print. Yet Yourcenar's *Memoirs of Hadrian* has sold almost a million copies since its publication in 1951 – an astounding figure for an intellectually demanding historical novel – and Yourcenar was the first woman to be elected to the prestigious French Academy, limited to 40 'Immortals' (the word used of those elected).

Yourcenar possessed a deep historical imagination. Over a long life she wrote dozens of books, mostly historical novels set in the ancient and Renaissance worlds, as well as short stories, plays and memoirs. Her distinction, however, was not limited to writing. She was also a thoroughly original personality who made the discovery of her own character her life's work. Her early years were spent immersed in ancient mythology and literature. Under different biographical circumstances she could have become one of Europe's great female classicists. Yet her imagination could not be confined to the factual realm. Instead it drove her to blend erudition with personal experience and transform the two into fiction, poetry and drama in a large literary output over seven decades from the 1920s to the 1980s. Philosophically she was a pessimist who believed that the human condition had changed little over the centuries. To demonstrate her belief she wrote about tormented characters, often based on real men in history, whose lives confirmed her pessimism. In so doing she became one of the preeminent historical novelists of the 20th century.

Yourcenar also explored the mysteries of same-sex love at a time when it was iconoclastic to do so. She had a deep understanding of same-sex female attachment, but she routinely configured as *male* the protagonists of her major works – Alexis, Hadrian, Antinous, Zeno, Mishima and other illustrious men. The reasons for this choice were complex. Her father had craved a son who would be famous. He bore a son, Marguerite's half-brother who grew up to be a complete failure. When Marguerite was born many years later her father reared her in the image of that wish. She imagined herself, in part, as *male* – a *famous* male – and specifically as a male author writing about other *male* figures. As she matured she came to believe that women in history had been far less interesting than men, so she wrote primarily about men and about *homosexual*, or bisexual, men. By the end of her writing career, in the early 1980s, it became apparent that she would be remembered as a homosexual writer of an unusual type. For her bravery in commemorating same-sex love – principally among powerful men – many readers admired her, especially during the repressive decades in America and Europe after World War Two. By the 1970s, Yourcenar had become a cultural icon, especially in France.

In literature Yourcenar's achievement is twofold: on the one hand, a perfection of style and form, on the other, a vivid historical imagination enabling her to convey her pessimistic view of the human condition. Each of her two accomplishments appears deceptively simple. Yourcenar's prose style (all her works were written in French) is sculpted, bare, well-wrought, often lapidary. She revised literary forms – whether the long historical novel, the novella, the short story, or the essay – to such a degree as to seem to elevate them to a science of style. But she did not break out of the mould of Romanticism, of which she was a latter-day representative. She was aware, of course, of the Modernist movement of her day, but she never innovated like Joyce, Woolf, Beckett, Stein or Cocteau. Formal experimentation was alien to her classical aesthetic and romantic sense of character. She was a writer firmly entrenched in the realist mode of Tolstoy, Thomas Mann, Chekhov, Conrad and – in France – Proust, Gide and Henri Montherlant.

Marguerite Yourcenar at home in Maine 1955

Yourcenar was deeply engaged in history, the strongest catalyst to her already ardent imagination. History, especially of the ancient and Renaissance world, grounded her pessimism and gave it shape by suggesting figures she could reclaim as heroic: the Roman Emperors Hadrian, Trajan, Marcus Aurelius and the fictional Zeno, a brilliant pastiche of several real and imaginary figures from the 16th century. Her working practice was to immerse herself for years – even decades – in the culture of an historical epic. Then she filtered this knowledge into the making of a single figure – usually male – who was paradoxically both representative and unrepresentative of this fabric. She removed herself from the scene and, by a kind of ventriloquism, permitted the figure to speak for himself – in the case of Hadrian, actually narrate his own life in the first person.

How did she sink so rapidly into obscurity? After her death

there was a flurry of writing about the nature of her achievement, especially after her unexpected election as the first woman to the French Academy, culminating, in 1991, in the massive biography[2] which assembles the known facts, year by year, except for what will be gleaned in 2037 when the closed file of her wartime papers at Harvard University will be opened.

Now less than two decades after her death in 1987, relatively few voices trumpet Yourcenar's greatness. When they do, they often do not say why. Even her most acclaimed works – *Memoirs of Hadrian*, *The Abyss*, the various volumes of her autobiography – are barely read today and rarely studied in colleges and universities. Some share in the neglect is owing to the academics who claim they discover nothing iconoclastic in her work. More pointedly, her reputation has suffered at the hands of some feminist critics, who accuse her of treachery to the feminist cause for celebrating the amours of ancient Greek males rather than modern women in love. Women of the last generation, expecting another Virginia Woolf, Radclyffe Hall, Sylvia Townsend Warner, or at least a second-rank Edith Wharton, were loath to embrace an author who seemed to be a hypocritical misogynist: proclaiming, as she does, that women could not be the subject of great literature while coveting women herself.[3] A recent estimate makes the point in brief: 'she is not a lesbian writer, she does not choose women as heroes, she does not celebrate same-sex love'.[4]

For these critics Yourcenar betrays her sex by failing to choose women as her protagonists. Hadrian, Zeno, Alexis and Nathanaël: all are men. The protagonists of her majestic didactic essays are male: Michelangelo, Dürer, Ruysdael, the Enlightenment Piranesi, Thomas Mann, heroic Romans and others. The authors she most revered (Euripides, Pindar) and the writers she translated (Cavafy, Henry James) were men, as were the majority of those who influenced her. Even the female ancestors she traced and reconstructed in her memoirs about her aristocratic origins

(*Dear Departed*) are portrayed as shadowy creatures compared to the stalwart men. Her distant cousins, the 19th-century brothers Octave and Rémo Pirmez – one became the foremost Belgian essayist of his epoch, the other an impassioned idealist who committed suicide at 28 – are brilliantly depicted at novel length. But stepmother Fernande, their younger sister, is a lugubrious and pathetic creature plainly longing for death. In brief, the argument is that Yourcenar is a woman who is a man. 'Being Hadrian' could have served as her just epitaph.

Recently, however, the tide has begun to turn. We capture Yourcenar as she comes into her own, just past her centenary: 1903–2003. The repeated academic cavil that she could not innovate in literary form is only part of the total picture: she was neither avant-garde nor surrealist, cubist nor dadaist, but her literary forms owe something magisterial to the European visual heritage from the era of Dürer and Dutch still-life to the post-Romantic painters of her own generation. Sight, more than other senses, captured and stimulated her imagination. (Smell and touch are less important; sound figures least, and despite listening to music and commenting on Bach she seems hardly to have been moved by most classical music.) She marvelled at paintings. She identified most with Rembrandt's *Polish Rider* among many and this in a curious but bewildering way: was it, one wonders, the rider's gaze or genderless pose?[5] She paused at seascapes in Maine, and wrote about life on the edge of their crashing waves. Some of her most expansive essays are devoted not to writers but to classical artists: Breughel, Ruysdael, Piranesi, Dürer and Rembrandt (in *The Dark Brain of Piranesi*). *The Abyss* started life as a story 'In the Manner of Dürer'.

Her debt to painting exceeds simple reference to these artists: it embeds their aesthetic principles into her narratives.[6] Yourcenar's writing imagination was highly visual: she uses words like a painter, first applying paint to a canvas, then standing back and commenting on what she has painted. One readily grasps, for example, how Dürer's classicism – his sense of proportion and perspective – gave rise to the depiction of her own characters. His figures, especially his males, are geometrically perfect, if static. Yourcenar also knew how to draw on Rembrandt's inspiration for movement in character development. Even in juvenescent travel she had been attracted to landscapes south of the Alps in Italy, Albania, Greece where visual scenes fired her historical imagination. She attributed an aspect of this passion to her Flemish origins in the land of the great painters. Her classicism was based on principles of proportion and the proper perspective into which each character had to be placed, as if in a Flemish tapestry. Hers was classicism purified of all excess and grotesque traits. Her visual sense does not render her an original novelist of the stature of Proust or Joyce, but the charge about the lack of innovation is being overthrown at this very moment.

Had Yourcenar fictionalized Sapphic loves instead of Hadrianic attachments, she might have broken through the Anglo-American barrier of neglect despite her Flemish origins and refusal to write originally anything in English. But, here too, the tide is gradually turning as diverse critics acknowledge that she was – of course – a lesbian writer but merely cast of another die. Yourcenar had her Alice Toklas, like Gertrude Stein, as we shall see, with whom she lived in conjugal intimacy. But she held a different view of life, art and sex – especially sexual ambiguity. She loved women and seduced them aggressively, but turned elsewhere than to the present time and the world of women for the substance of many of her fictions.

For Yourcenar it is history and the immutable realities of the human condition, rather than the random chance of biological gender, that remain the clue to unlocking the mystery of her identity and quest. She would identify a problem in the human condition – for example, the role of the occult – and then seek to locate it in an historical moment when the issue was temporarily salient, in this case the Renaissance. This process, back and forth, formed the basis of a lifelong process she dubbed *opening my eyes*. They opened in present time but affixed themselves to a retrievable past. Both present (experience) and past (learning) were necessary for a great writer. There was no other way to comprehend the unchanging, eternal human condition. This is what it meant to be a classicist: not merely in possession of a sculpted style but a writer who extracted fundamental humanity in the human predicament.

Yourcenar was a strong personality: confident in her abilities, ambitious for her own career, persuaded she was important, fiercely secretive, and dedicated to her art. She conducted herself in public as if prying into her secrets would be tantamount to violation. Yet the lives and works of great artists cannot be separated out: each feeds the other. Yourcenar's life existed in exquisite, tantalizing proximity to her work – one reason she so consciously aimed to remove herself from her fictions. Her goal was to write almost as if she had never existed, as if she were merely the angelic observer who had reconstructed the truth –

Yourcenar at the ceremony for the Prix Femina in 1953

STRONG PERSONALITY

as if the squat, fat, unprepossessing French woman, barely over five feet, with a twinkle in her knowing eye, had been composed of unalloyed spirit.

Marguerite Antoinette Jeanne Marie Ghislaine de Crayencour was born on 8 June 1903 at 193 Avenue Louise in Brussels. (Yourcenar is an anagram she herself formed from the ten letters of her father's name, dropping the second c.) Marguerite went to no schools but was educated in her father's oak-panelled library at Mont Noir, in French Flanders. Her mother Fernande was Belgian, her father – Michel de Cleenewerck de Crayencour – French. At Mont Noir she learned Greek and Latin and other modern languages (English, German, Italian and some Spanish) in Michel's lap.

Her father's favourite, Marguerite made him into a heroic, larger-than-life figure, not merely idolizing him but imagining him as the scion of an ancient family whose rise and fall from the Middle Ages she alone was destined to retrieve in her memoirs. Her earliest attachments were to her father, who instilled in her two beliefs: first, that she was destined for greatness no matter what the fates decreed; second, that she had lost nothing by not being born male.

As she grew to adulthood, Marguerite came to sense a tension between her father's aspirations and her pressing sensual desires. Unable to confront these demons head on, she travelled during her 20s, nomadically and profusely, searching for herself. Her father died in 1929, when she was 26. She continued to crisscross Europe's girth, falling in and out of love with men and simultaneously seducing women.

One day in February 1939, almost by serendipity, she met Grace Frick (1903–79), the daughter of an American family in Kansas City (no relation to the wealthy Fricks of the famous Frick Gallery in New York City) in a Paris hotel. Each recognized something attractive in the other, perhaps even intuited what their friendship augured. Other travels intervened before Yourcenar could visit her in America. But when she did, within a few years they found themselves setting up house on Mount Desert Island off the north coast of Maine where they cohabited until Grace's death, four decades later, in 1979. Together they forged the image the world received of two courageous women struggling against the elements on the northwestern edge of the brutal ocean. There Yourcenar spent more than half her 84 years in writerly seclusion, suggesting to some observers that she was as American as she was French.

Without Grace Frick, Yourcenar could not have achieved so much. Frick read and translated much that Yourcenar wrote. She kept the time-wasters at bay so that her partner could get on with her writing, and provided the money, at first. She continued to serve as the perpetual guardian and unflinching monitor of their retreat. She organized Marguerite's daily routine, enabling her to cope with life's rigours by guiding her through its mundane logistics.

Grace also indulged 'Madame's' (the nickname Yourcenar encouraged for herself) illnesses. Her beloved was a bona fide hypochondriac, routinely ill with aches of the head and elsewhere, fevers and pains. Peaks of manic activity would be followed by troughs of depression. Marguerite's moods were legion. No case history exists but a rigorous study would demonstrate that her illnesses were protective and self-sustaining.[7] Grace understood them and selflessly took them on board. When she herself became a chronic patient after she contracted breast cancer during the last decade of her life, she grew even more indulgent. Yourcenar's hypochondria would not be noteworthy if it did not directly nourish her rituals of writing. Like the Virginia Woolf she translated, she seemed to think a writer had to be ill to survive the fever of composition.

Grace Frick at Yale University 1936

Yet it is tempting to speculate whether Yourcenar would have remained attached to Grace had she not been so propitious for her career. What might Yourcenar's life have been like if she had not coupled up with Grace or if, having coupled up, she had left her – as she was often tempted to do? Yourcenar would never have removed herself to Mount Desert alone, or, once there, remained. Her return to her nomadic life after Grace's death proves as much. Grace had what Yourcenar needed when they became a couple in the 1940s, not least money. Marguerite was virtually homeless (Michel having bankrupted the family estate) and longing for someone, though not necessarily a conjugal same-sex partner, who could convert her penchant for seduction and travel into the discipline necessary to become a writer. In 1949 Marguerite was willing; 30 years later, in 1979, when Grace had just died, she was less certain the choice had been right.

Yourcenar's alteration after Grace's death was fundamentally one of routine and diminished productivity: she wrote less and the words no longer came easily. Instead she gave herself up to reckless travel. She was approaching 80, but was still sufficiently vital to commence global travels again as she had in her youth, this time with a male American photographer a third her age. Jerry Wilson had travelled to Mount Desert to interview her in 1978 and never parted from her until his own death from AIDS seven years later. This last decade of Yourcenar's life resembled her third and fourth in the 1920s and 1930s when she was determined to discover for herself whether the places she had read about lived up to her imagination of them. Now, with Jerry, her travels entailed nostalgia and the recognition of familiar places revisited after a long interval during which she had become world famous.

Yourcenar voyaged with Jerry back and forth over the Atlantic, until she herself was too tired to go any more. Their union had been far from peaceful. Fights erupted, patched up by apologies, but nothing could cancel the reality that she was tired and he was young. Rarely has a woman of her age travelled so widely and with seduction in mind with a nubile (from the photographs one could also say gorgeous) male a third her age. Her bravado in flaunting him in Europe's capitals was legendary: she had never experienced any of this frisson with Grace who some took for a factotum, others for a lackey or valet.

Grace's death had nevertheless been a huge loss, Jerry's another, in relatively quick succession. Once Jerry was gone, a new loneliness set in caused by lack of regular conversation among those few intimates with whom she could be herself. 'Being herself' also entailed the continuing possibility, despite age and incipient decrepitude, of the seduction of others. Somewhere in her prolific correspondence of those years after Jerry's death she wrote: *With Jerry, I had grown used to the delight of speaking my own language all day long, and suddenly I had to wait for friends to drop by in order to do so.*[8] This latter-day seduction by the octogenarian retained its fleshy edge, partook of the sexual dimension every bit as forcefully as the youthful predator hunting her game during the 1930s. Still, conversation had formed one of the pillars of her life. As the locals used to say up on Mount Desert, 'Madame speaks the same as she writes books.'[9]

The void after Jerry's death seemed unbearable and in 1987 her health deteriorated. Marguerite had a series of fatal strokes and died on 17 December 1987 on the island where she had immured herself for five decades.

'Nautilus Island's hermit heiress lives high above the sea,' New England poet Robert Lowell once exclaimed in *Life Studies* of another reclusive poet; he could equally have been describing Marguerite's life with Grace. Yourcenar needed some remote spot where she could think and dream and write undisturbed. Not that she was a hermit or an Arcadian, but to live in Paris or another world-class city for six more decades would have been unthinkable. Yourcenar's retreat with her lover to a frozen and somewhat desolate place is one part of her success as a writer and explains something about her relationship with the powerful patriarchs of past and present – Hadrian, Zeno, Piranesi, Thomas Mann, Mishima – who also secluded and isolated themselves and with whom she was constantly comparing herself in the life of her mind. Yourcenar's hypochondria craved geographical isolation. It is easier to provide care to the self – and so enjoy the psychological protections that hypochondria offers – away from the maddening crowd where one is watched.

Yet Marguerite and Grace were less willingly reclusive than they seemed. Marguerite needed solitude to write, but their financial plight was at least as strong a motive: she and Grace could live on a shoestring on Mount Desert. Yourcenar was a free agent in every way except fiscally. Apart from the 12 years she spent as a part-time lecturer at Sarah Lawrence College in upstate New York, where she kept herself far removed from internal academic politics, she never worked for anyone else. She craved the life of a woman of belles-lettres, beholden to no one except her own conscience. Their great friend Natalie Barney sent Marguerite cheques. Extroverted like Marguerite, primarily lesbian, equally histrionic and flamboyant, Barney lavished thousands on herself and her friends in her Paris salon at number 20 on the rue Jacob.

Midnight séances, candlelit soirées and caviar suppers were generously served up to other feminists. Yourcenar and Frick, in contrast, survived meagrely in Maine, scraping together whatever little profit they could for travel. Barney, well aware that her writer-friend across the ocean lived quietly as much out of need as for any other reason, continued to send Yourcenar cheques for many years until her death in 1962.

The myth of the recluse also enlarged allied tales about Yourcenar's aloofness and fierce dislike of men whom she judged paradoxically to be her intellectual inferiors. It is true that she generally got on better with women than men and, though she had many male friends, they were generally adulators who, as it were, worshipped in her temple. But the view of her as a man-hater, like the myth about her as a hermit, is largely false. More than anything, her hardness came from her discipline as a writer. She worked to schedule and possessed remarkable powers of concentration. She obeyed deadlines, even when they were her own, and she compulsively revised, compressed and polished. But once finished, she returned to far-flung travels, friends, indulging both sentiment and hedonism. That was the image she had forged of herself and she worked hard to make it a reality.

To the end of her days Marguerite wrote prolific correspondence, which must figure into any estimate of her stature as a figure in the history of letters.[10] Letters had served multiple purposes: trading information from an outpost of urban civilization, keeping her in touch with her French publishers, whether confirming their views or excoriating them, paving the way for Europeans to visit her in good weather, as well as allowing her to find her truest voices and construct an autobiographical record with an eye to the future of her image.[11] Her letters are sculpted: each is a coherent document in its own right, partaking of the same spare, direct style as her books. They form an important part of the Gallo-American literary history of the 20th century.

Yourcenar's relations with publishers – in Paris Gallimard, Grasset, Plon, in America Farrar Straus – were so remarkably fraught and litigious they should figure into any history of publishing in the last century. Yourcenar relished battles and lawsuits and played one publisher off another for higher royalties, retaining lawyers in Paris solely to represent her in her feuds. She warred with their heads of houses: Claude Gallimard, Bernard Grasset, Georges Poupet at Plon, Roger Straus, not merely delegates or representatives. And she fought from a vast geographical distance at a time when communications were less predictable than they are now. Fearless from afar, she braved the long waits and emotional stress. The sums involved remain murky. She paid her lawyers and must have had sufficient funds from her royalties to retain them. Or did Frick also contribute? This financial conundrum has major implications for her partnered life with Grace. When, for example, did she first have sufficient means from her royalties to leave Grace in the way she had fantasized for so long?

Yourcenar's wars with her publishers reveal the tenacious fibre of which she was hewn. Even she conceded that she was not always in the right but she would not be cowed: prideful she ploughed ahead, challenging them in detailed epistles all the way to the courts. Financial reward played a part, of course, but money was not the sole determinant; she had to believe the publisher had feted her, appreciated her gifts, treated her like the queen-bee author she willed herself to become. She was haughty and grand – though not everyone saw the same aspect of her. Some of the islanders in Maine, for example, presumed she was a prodigy of learning who had descended to their backwoods community, others that she was merely a stranger who spoke poor English. She did not indulge fools, especially among her publishers: the mainstay of her living and the linchpin of the international reputation she was forging. Her poised, almost imperial manner seemed to possess ultimate self-belief. Yet hauteur also served her as armour:

as a shield designed more to support her own confidence than attack others.

Grace's death in 1979 resulted in the loss of Yourcenar's main translator into English, the only one who had been at her side, day in and day out for almost 40 years. There were others – Harvard Professor Walter Kaiser, Richard Howard, Dori Katz, Arthur Goldhammer, Edith R Farrell, David Freeman, Alberto Manguel and, after Yourcenar's death, Maria Louise Ascher – waiting in the wings. She wrote nothing originally in English; so fierce was her loyalty to the mother tongue where she thought her truest talents lodged. Yet she kept a vigilant eye to ensure speedy English translations, aware that her reputation in a predominantly English-speaking world would be made that way. She laboured towards perfection with her translators, passing on every detail and nuance. But the renditions of her English translators vary immensely and her prose is far more accomplished in French than in any English translation. In French she could practise the restrained classicism (principles of stylistic balance, proportion, a Spartan economy of style and symmetry) and stylistic dignity she cultivated.

Yourcenar was a compulsive reviser, not merely continuously rewriting entire works but rethinking their original conception. Her custom was to imagine her books long before she set pen to paper. Later she would make notes and lock them away. Later yet – sometimes after decades – something would occur to remind her of the long forgotten original imagining or set of notes she had made. She relocated them or reinvented the original idea; then she set out to write. Once at work she could write quickly, but it took years for her ideas to mellow and take shape into literary forms. Just as with the French wines she drank, she construed a few decades of ageing as de rigueur. Her major works – *Memoirs of Hadrian*, *The Abyss*, *A Coin in Nine Hands*, *Dear Departed*, *Mishima*, even the relatively youthful *Alexis* – were composed in this slow, sedimentary way. She gained confidence by not rushing into print but rather having time to stand back and comment on her own processes of composition. Her books were like vials of her life: their droplets slowly dripped out over the time allotted to her. Of course, only an author privileged to write over many decades – Yourcenar's career stretched over seven, starting in the 1920s and continuing until she had no more to say in the 1980s – has this luxury.

Her religion, like so many of the other contradictions in her life and works, was more complex than its Catholic roots suggest. Religion, in Stoical and hermetic versions, routinely features in her historical fictions, but not Christianity. Wilfully she reconstructed the religious mindsets of her pagan protagonists but she herself rarely attended church, nor do her Christian characters. Hadrian, Zeno and the Prior of the Cordeliers in *The Abyss* all worship gods whose presence Yourcenar felt acutely, despite her secularism. One could claim she herself was paradoxically both a Stoic, believing happiness comes from balance, and a hedonist, believing that happiness comes through excess: Stoic as the natural consequence of her entrenched pessimism, hedonist because all forms of sensuality excited and tempted her. Insofar as she was a Christian, she was a Stoic one, persuaded that the human condition was too cruel to benefit much from sentiment. These conflicting gods, both Christian and classical, led her to value the hybrid explorations of alchemical religion and she read several of their expounders – Paracelsus, Campanella, Giordano Bruno, and such modern devotees as Jung and Kerényi.

Someone so exceptionally pessimistic by temperament was destined to become immersed in death. Marguerite had been caught in its claws for a long time. The more death haunted her, the more she worked at the objective perfection of her writer's craft and yearned for a classic style that could live on after her demise. In some fundamental sense she perceived herself as alive only as her major protagonists, Hadrian, Zeno, Alexis. She referred to them and their sayings years after each book had been published, writing about them as if she herself had assumed the mantle of their lives or as if, having died herself, she had joined them in the underworld. Dostoevsky's works, especially his *House of the Dead*, spoke to her, as did Tolstoy's epic novels and those of the other Russian realists who made death into a problem and theorized about it. It is not simply that death fascinated her. She also possessed an intuitive sense that wise sages and other heroic patriarchs – always men – fastidiously prepare themselves for death. Their scrupulous arrangements constitute some of her most vivid writing, as in the last section of the *Memoirs of Hadrian*, which many readers continue to think the most accomplished part of the book, surpassing her descriptions of his love for, and mourning after, Antinous's death. Her own death was less philosophical but no less well prepared: travelled out, worn down, an ailing midoctogenarian, she had already sorted the archive destined for Harvard and cultivated her official biographer.[12]

Yourcenar conceptualized virtually all her major themes in the early part of her life, before she came to America. Maine, after 1949, provided her a writer's sequestration free of cares that could have distracted her, but not the ideas themselves. These arose in Europe, especially around the southern Mediterranean, in the time between the two great wars, which she called her *Greek and Italian period*.[13] Here she trod common ground with the ancients in the cradle of their unparalleled civilization. She remained a European to the core, conceived in the nest of the French language and its mentalities. Nothing in America ever changed her mind. She never warmed to America, nor America to her, no matter how fond she was of swashbuckling natives like Jerry Wilson and his boyfriends, no matter how many African-American spirituals she translated into French.

The nomadism already mentioned functioned on several levels for Yourcenar. It allowed her to seek far-flung places to develop a much-needed context for her imaginings about her biographical self and her fictional inventions. Travel also paved the way for her seductions of both men and women. She encountered people easily, in train stations and hotels and on street corners where she engaged them in enchanting conversation and invited them up for a drink. Later on, in the midstream of life, travel over many months served yet another purpose, as a counterpoint to weeks of intensely concentrated writing, a switch-off to its solitariness. This was true in Europe before she migrated to America; the habit intensified in Maine. By her mid-50s regular travel had become such an ingrained way of life that she craved it as if addicted. This is why she travelled so compulsively in her last decade in the 1980s. Not to travel was tantamount to death.

She imported her wanderlust into her literature, not merely amongst the tragic literary giants she set out to depict – Gide, Cavafy, Mann – but also her historical heroes and family relations. Each travels widely: Hadrian through his Roman Empire from Iberia to the steppes of the Caucasus, Zeno in middle Europe. Even the Pirmez brothers, her cousins Octave and Rémo, who figure so brilliantly as the centrepiece of *Dear Departed*, are presented as *Two Travellers Bound for the Realm Immutable* despite their having travelled less than she did.[14] Yourcenar captures Roman Hadrian brilliantly on these ventures, as on the fatal one during which Antinous drowns in the Nile. These are men travelling with other men: pro-consuls, vassals, priors, sorcerers, even Cyprian the sodomite, one of Zeno's assistants in *The Abyss*. The writer is the odd woman out and seemed to imagine herself among their company, another male.

> Gustave Flaubert in young manhood: 'There are days when one longs to be a woman.' Gustave in maturity: 'Madame Bovary, c'est moi.'
>
> Julian Barnes, *Flaubert's Parrot*[15]

Our lady craved the reverse: Hadrian, c'est moi. Yourcenar wrote what is often called in contemporary analysis cross-dressed narratives, in which the writer assumes the guise of the opposite gender, or disguises characters in the opposite sex: Albert for Albertine in Proust for example. Yourcenar engages in both. She is a woman writing about men and her men are not cross-dressed – they *are* males – but in a convoluted way she nevertheless writes about women in love. From her notion that women cannot be the subjects of serious literature she has arrived at an aesthetic in which she readily transposes them into men, and, having done so, she is satisfied that she has not abandoned her inner quest to understand what Wilde had called in *De Profundis* 'the love that hath no name'.

We will look closely at this dimension of gender in her oeuvre. Not in any narrowly literal way (to comprehend, for example, how she, a biological female, imagined the physical reality of the young Roman lover Antinous), but rather to understand in more general terms how and why she cross-gendered her narratives: asking what her conception was of women in these historical epochs (ancient Greece, ancient Rome, the Reformation and so on) and how she went about psychologically imagining women in love as *men in love* before removing herself at the end of the imaginative process to lend an impression that all she had done was reconstruct the historical love of (for example) Hadrian and Antinous. All of which returns us to those feminists who dismiss her from the canon of lesbian writers and claim that she could not openly celebrate women in love. The sexual dimension is restrained and adroitly disguised but nevertheless present in all her writing. In *Alexis* she confronts same-sex love directly; elsewhere she covers her narratives in veils disguising the underlying gender identity of her figures.

These four themes – classicism, nomadism, erotic lust and cross-gendered writing (especially as the basis for the greatest human tragedies) – shall constitute the heart of this biographical account, for they lead to the centre of Yourcenar country. She will not be consistent in her positions or present the four coherently. The contradictions in, and tensions of, her own life are mirrored in her writing. Strategic decisions in her books often reflect her ambivalence. Still, the pattern is there from start to finish: male protagonists, almost always in love with other males, compelled to wander, often to flee the prison house of their sexualities, all in the equipoise of the writer's most controlled classicism. There is no hypocrisy here, just the contradictions and incommensurables inherent in the artistic enterprise.

The following chapters highlight these four themes within the larger purpose of conveying a sense of her distinctive personality – as cerebral as it could be sensuous – while exploring the personas of her fiction. As we follow the unfolding of her life, each theme follows from the other, despite overlaps and reciprocities: the early classicism which became entrenched as she matured; her avidity as seductress and traveller; death as the natural extension of erotic love; and finally the extraordinary liberation she experienced after Grace's death – Grace who had been her greatest benefactor on earth. How can these contradictions have been so passionately combined?

Passionate Classicist: 1903–1929

Yourcenar remembered the most extraordinary aspect of her childhood as its *classlessness*,[16] but the family's rural seat at Mont Noir outside the village of Saint-Jans-Cappel, in northeastern France, close to the Belgian border, was also beautiful, idyllic and socially privileged. It was sold in 1912, when she was nine, and then torn down, but there is no reason to distrust the child's memory of her first years. Female relations came and went: aunts, grandmothers (the ferocious Noémi, Michel's mother), a German governess called 'Fraulein', who Marguerite came to imagine was her father's lover. Marguerite's mother Fernande died aged 31 from complications of pregnancy ten days after the birth of her first and only child, on 8 June 1903.[17] Everything we know of Michel's reaction to Fernande's death comes from Yourcenar herself and is explained in *Dear Departed*, especially the sense that if Michel was profoundly shaken and distressed, he nevertheless did not grieve.

Michel was now 50, a widower for the second time in four years and a compulsive gambler. Tall, still dashing, rail-thin, he looked like someone who had just stepped out of a Merry-Widower operetta, complete with his straw boater, handlebar moustache with rounded curlicues on each end, wing-tipped collars and slight chin (the French call it a *menton fuyant* – an evasive chin). Berthe, his first wife, had died in 1899, leaving him with a 17-year old son, Michel, whom he intensely disliked. His reasons were complex and had as much to do with his dislike of Berthe as of their progeny. They are germane here only to the degree that they freed him to dote on the new baby. It would be another 23 years, not until 1926, when he was 73, just three years before his death, that he married for the third, and last, time. For now, he devoted himself entirely to Marguerite, his hobbies – especially while travelling– and his frequent romantic flings.

The toddler preferred reciting poetry to playing with other children, which did not endear her to any, and soon she found herself with few children she could call friends. Michel somehow filled the void and swept her off her feet. Yourcenar has written at great length about him in *How Many Years*. They quickly became equals, friends rather than kin, despite the great age difference. It tickled her to have such an authority figure all to herself in the big house. His blend of characteristics – his gallantry as a former soldier, his old-world charm, his charisma, which she labours to locate but ends admitting she cannot – attracted her more than anything. He read to her, walked with her and discussed with her. No mother intruded. More than anything she remembered how they used *to walk for hours, talking about Greek philosophy or Shakespeare or Swedish stories; sometimes about things he had remembered or stories he'd heard from people still older than himself.*[18] This was the *summum bonum* of love. Marguerite never forgot what she had had in her first decade of life.

We saw a good deal of London, the National Gallery, the British Museum. There I saw Hadrian for the first time, a virile, almost brutal, bronze depicting the emperor at age forty or so, which had been fished out of the Thames in the nineteenth century, and I also saw the Elgin marbles.

With Open Eyes[19]

Mont Noir was sold in 1912, as the precocious little girl approached ten. Michel concluded the sale, moved the household to central Paris and then left to travel. In 1914 he returned and took her to England for the year – just the two of them. Their ferryboat was intercepted by the Germans as they tried to return to France, so they remained in Richmond near London and only went back to Paris a year later, in the thick of war.

Michel rented a flat in a 19th-century house with a majestic courtyard on the rue d'Antin, hired servants, and continued to teach the young girl himself. It was in the heart of the theatre district in the second arrondissement, where the plays of Racine and Corneille had been performed. Marguerite learned their frontages and marquees well, thinking she might become a famous playwright someday. She never outgrew the electric charge of wandering through the theatre district of France's capital. This period was also notable for its innovations in the visual arts — expressionism, cubism and the beginnings of surrealism — but Marguerite had no attraction to the canvas despite her great admiration of painting. Later on, she would write as if painting with the brush. But for now she bought dozens of classic French plays, read them and watched their performances a few hundred yards from their flat and occasionally on the Left Bank in the Théâtre Sarah-Bernhardt or in the Théâtre de la Potinière where sexually explicit plays were performed in English. Father and daughter remained there throughout the war, enduring the cold and warming themselves in the nearby museums where Marguerite's early taste for the visual was rekindled.

The apartment lay between the Opera and Royal Palace, just

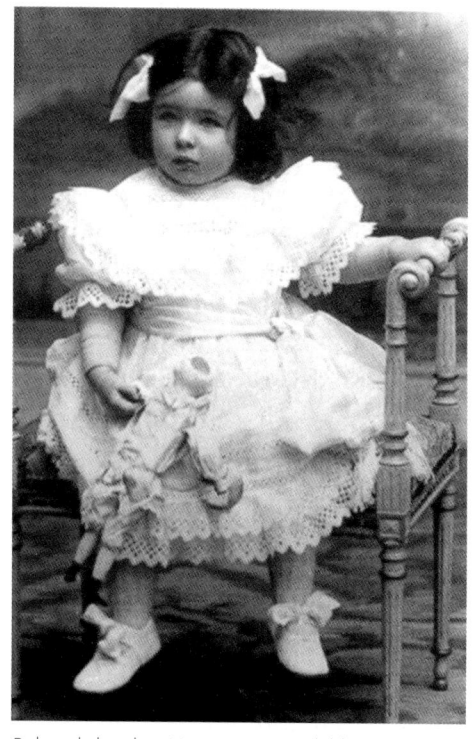

Beloved daughter Yourcenar as a child in 1905

American Sylvia Beach (1887–1967), owner of Shakespeare & Co on Paris's Left Bank, privately printed James Joyce's *Ulysses* in April 1921 and sold it by subscription. Her bookshop was frequented by writers including Hemingway, Joyce, Pound, Fitzgerald, John Dos Passos, Henry Miller, e e cummings and Gertrude Stein. She remained there throughout the 1930s as the clouds of the Nazi menace gathered. Her American clientele fled the war, and her bookshop was closed early in the 1940s. After the German occupation of Paris Beach was sent to an internment camp, but by 1944 was back on the rue Odéon as Allied troops arrived to liberate the city. After the war she continued to run Shakespeare & Co until her death in 1967, holding frequent book readings and cultural programmes. Marguerite bought many books from her in the 1920s. Three decades later, in the winter of 1952, when the *Memoirs of Hadrian* had just appeared, Marguerite returned there: not to promote her new book, which had not yet been translated into English and could therefore not be sold in the shop carrying English titles only, but to participate in an evening displaying high-society fashion clothing.

above the colourful Marché St Honoré with its vegetables and raw fish. It was an easy stroll to the Tuileries Gardens and Louvre and if you crossed over Pont des Arts upon emerging from the Louvre, as Marguerite often did after looking at the pictures, you entered the Left Bank on the Quai de Conti, where Marguerite would be immortalized over a half century later. On days when she continued further along the Odéon towards the National Theatre she walked to Sylvia Beach's bookshop at 21 rue Odéon to browse her fabulous assortment of English books.

Money was not abundant but they had sufficient means, even for Michel's flings and trips to Monte Carlo. Marguerite had already frequented the London museums and was now, during the Great War, becoming an habitué of the Louvre and its surrounding galleries. She was reading in six languages (French, Italian, German, Flemish, Dutch and English) by the time she was 15. She became fluent in these and other languages and spoke them throughout her life. Her reading included Euripides, Aristophanes, Chateaubriand, Goethe, Maeterlinck, Shakespeare, Racine, La Bruyère, Ibsen, Nietzsche, Tolstoy (especially his 'Kreutzer Sonata'), Huysmans and Romain Rolland. In her reading now the novelists were first; then came the poets, especially Hugo and the 17th-century poets in both French and English, which she read in the original. The different styles of these authors made an impression on the teenager, especially when she began to write draft novels and plays a few years later, by 1927. It was evident that her writing was already, at this tender age, tough and lucidly sane. She came upon Oriental literature herself, especially the Japanese Noh plays. Michel read aloud to her the trilogies of the mystical Russian novelist Dmitri Sergeyevich Merezhkovsky and the anti-Semitic, ultranationalist French writer Michel Barrès, both then in vogue, the latter especially so. She avoided Balzac and Flaubert, largely because they were no favourites of Michel. When Marguerite demanded that they be included Michel succumbed, at least for Flaubert, who was read aloud. Gide she followed for her own reasons and was more influenced by him than she was ever to admit. By her own testimony she came late to Proust (around 1927) and later still to Dostoevsky who *took away my breath*.[20]

> *If you're looking for influences, you'd probably do better to look to the philosophers. It would be impossible to overestimate Nietzsche's influence, for example: the Nietzsche not of* Zarathustra *but of* Joyful Wisdom *and* Human, All Too Human, *the Nietzsche who had a certain way of looking at things, from close up and at the same time from afar, a man lucid and acute as a writer yet light of touch.*
>
> With Open Eyes[21]

She read Nietzsche as a teenager, as well as Schopenhauer, who made a profound impression on her by introducing her to the wisdom of Buddhism and the true meaning of despair. These authors sat well with her already pessimistic, philosophical cast of mind. During these formative years (1915–25) living in Paris with Michel mystical religion also became important for her. It was intellectual and aesthetic religion rather than the church-going type. She came to it through her inherited Catholicism; but it had always been the ritual rather than the doctrine of Catholicism that impressed her. Yourcenar has commented on the origins of her mystical religion in many of her autobiographical works. They reduce to the same point: mystical ritual had acted as a type of cement, or glue, in history, binding past to present. It was the constant in the human psyche and accounted for its creative vision. This line of thinking is what gave her the idea, still as an adolescent, to write a small book about the ancient Greek poet Pindar. She began it by 1920 but did not publish it until 1932.

Her mind was formed primarily by studying languages, reading books and looking at objects in museums. She came to literature via poetry, then consumed novels with Michel; around 15 she added philosophy. Omitted was contemporary commentary: she and Michel dipped into few newspapers regularly and were uninterested in them. World War One made little impression on this adolescent. History was also a significant omission at this stage. She was steeped in the literature of the past: ancient, Renaissance, Romantic and of the generation just before hers in the *fin de siècle* but not the ephemeral literature of her own day, no matter how shell-shocking the world events to which it responded.

She began Greek and Latin before the age of ten. Ancient life – its customs, manners and ways of living – captured her attention as an adolescent. The Greek myths especially struck her in a profoundly personal way, and she was not alone. Survey the French literature written by the canonical writers of 1910 to 1930 and one quickly glimpses the degree to which the ancient Greek world continued to keep its stranglehold. She had seen the Greek gods painted on canvases in the Paris museums. It is therefore not surprising that her very first published work should have been a small book of poems on mythological themes entitled *The Garden of Illusions*. This she sent to several literary personalities, including the Indian poet Rabindranath Tagore, who wrote her two letters and invited her to stay in India. He also awakened in her an interest in the Persian poet-astronomer Omar Khayyám (1050–1123), which was almost to rival that in Emperor Hadrian.[22] The centrepiece is a long poem about the ascent of Icarus before he takes his fatal plunge. She had been as impressed by Breughel's painting of Icarus in the Louvre as the head of the Mondragone Antinous. How meaningful for her long career ahead that this piece of juvenilia, her first published work, should already capture the over-reaching gesture: the human spirit grasping towards great things in heaven.

The Icarus poem fell dead from the press – swooped to its sepulchre as quickly as its mythic original had. Yourcenar herself dispraised it, calling it a mistake.[24] It was followed within months by a set of short romantic poems: *The Gods are not Dead* (1922) dedicated to Michel's new English mistress, Christine Hoevelt. In those days upper-class French women like Marguerite routinely attended university but not with a father like Michel. Besides, Yourcenar was preoccupied with other matters: for one thing, her literary ambitions. In that same year, 1922, her 20th, she had sketched the first plan of what would eventually become her two masterpieces, *Memoirs of Hadrian*, then called *Antinous*, and her tale of Renaissance occultism, *The Abyss*, then called *Crosscurrents*. She recognized that her knowledge of ancient and Renaissance culture was too fragmented to complete

> *My father offered to pay for the publication of my Icarus poem as a sort of Christmas present, and he asked me if I preferred to publish under a pseudonym. I answer, 'Yes, of course.' . . . So we set about looking for a name and passed a pleasant evening making anagrams of the name Crayencour, moving words and letters around on a sheet of paper until we came up with the name Yourcenar. I'm very fond of the letter Y, which is such a beautiful letter.*
>
> With Open Eyes[23]

the book and, in 1921, converted *Crosscurrents* into three short stories, 'In the Manner of Dürer', 'In the Manner of El Greco', 'In the Manner of Rembrandt', giving them these titles to create the semblance of a unified collection despite their remaining unpublished. 'Rembrandt' contained the seeds of 'An Obscure Man', which she would publish almost 60 years later in 1982, almost unrecognizable from the original. 'Greco', also reworked, relates the incest of brother Miguel and sister Anna whose love affairs culminate during one Holy Week in Naples. Yourcenar finished it after her return to Paris from Italy in the spring of 1925. It gives great emphasis to its adolescent erotic thrusts and forms the original of *Anna, Soror*, based on the close bond between the Carthaginian sisters, Anna and Dido, in Virgil's *Aeneid*. Rewritten in a more mellow form almost 60 years later, it was collected in a volume called *Like the Water that Flows*. 'Dürer' was destined to become her second best-selling masterpiece, *The Abyss*, not published until 1968.

She was making other similarly precocious compositions. Comb the season 1921–22 and you have the origin of half of Yourcenar's major works. Conception and execution proceeded in this way: ideas sprang from classical or historical sources. Eros and ambition as hallmarks of the human condition combined to form two of their main themes. All plots were set in previous historical epochs. She often cast her figures as Dutchmen. Years later she speculated that there might be *a sensibility of the Low Countries, both Belgian and Dutch as well as French . . . a kind of visionary realism that I feel dwells in me.*[25] What she had

> *Every writer only carries within him a certain number of beings. Rather than representing the latter in the guise of new characters, which would hardly be anything but old characters with different first names, I have been more inclined to deepen, develop, and nourish those beings with whom I was already in the habit of living, getting to know them better as I have learned more about life and improving on a world that was already my own.*
>
> 'Reflections on the Composition of the *Memoirs of Hadrian*'[26]

imbibed from paintings was transported, unconsciously for the most part, into her narratives. She hatched an idea, wrote it out, published it in one version, then had no compunction in recasting it and renaming it many times in different forms. She found great wisdom in reworking old books over and over again, like pouring old wine into new flasks.

Everything she signed Yourcenar. Crayencour was gone. Except that her father Michel, though ageing, was still vibrant, frequently away on travels throughout Europe, alone or with his women. From him she acquired the faith that travel imparted experience, experience wisdom, and wisdom the stuff of writing. In 1922, when she was not yet 20, Michel took her to Venice, Milan and Verona for the first time. She was exhilarated that the Italian cities exceeded the beauties she had read about. A light had been kindled and she would return many times in the 1920s: Rome in 1924, Naples again in 1925, Florence, Rimini, and points further south.

She also read dense genealogical manuscripts about the Crayencours, not merely of the last few generations, but extending back into the Middle Ages, which Michel gave her during those years. They stuck in the recesses of her mind; she revived them many times in her autobiographical memoirs, especially in *Dear Departed*. Concurrently she was also slowly becoming preoccupied with her relations with women. Not merely the women about whom she was reading (Crayencour women) or writing (the incestuous Anna who practically rapes her little brother) but another woman, twice her age, Christine Hoevelt, whom Michel would marry a couple of years later, in 1926, at Marguerite's encouragement. Jealousy set in between them, but jealousy with a twist: she discovered herself both recoiling from and attracted to the woman. The continuing conflict in her mind energized her. On the one hand, she dedicated works to Christine and cultivated her as a stepmother; on the other she derogated her in Michel's eyes.

Also raging in her psyche was a philosophical debate about the differences between the lover and the beloved, even Michel and Christine when cast into these nebulous roles. Who was better off? Which received the greater pleasure? What were their dynamic differences? Who was playing which role? How could anyone be sure? She reached no conclusions and was distracted by Michel's failing health. He was now over 70 and had lived wantonly, squandering his property and fortune. Paris's winters were becoming unbearable for him and, by 1925, he had set up for part of each year in balmy Monte Carlo. The 22-year-old Marguerite followed him. There was nothing to keep her in Paris, neither boyfriends nor girlfriends. In Monte Carlo she could read in peace while enjoying the Mediterranean waves.

Two years and two or three months previously, when Michel was already ailing, he had taken a third wife, an Englishwoman. She was sentimental and conventional as only someone from the British middle class can be, but she cared for him devotedly . . . that Englishwoman who thought Dickens common and revered the upright families in Galsworthy's novels, believed in reconciliations between close relatives. Like many Britishers of modest means in those days, she had recently spent a number of years living in family boarding houses on the Continent, primarily in Belgium.

How Many Years[27]

She read biographies of historical figures in vogue and decided to write one herself, about the Greek lyric poet Pindar. But she underestimated the difficulty of the task: her Greek was insufficient to tackle this syntactically most abstruse of the ancient poets. It turned into a hard write, divided into three sections (youth, works, maturity and old age), a conventional chronological life. *Pindar* was not published until 1932, after her friend and editor André Fraigneau discovered it. She also composed short stories and published her first piece based on reading Oriental writers. She penned a 'Diagnostic of Europe' claiming that its standards of culture were deteriorating so appallingly as to turn the civilized world into a political morass.[28]

During these early rummages through the ancient past Marguerite was especially attracted by figures of sexual ambivalence who lived in epochs permitting maximum freedom. Such conflicted creatures included those who, perhaps like herself, loved too violently; or whose love was misunderstood or even violated. Henri III (1551–89), King of France in the 16th century – the period she was to return to many times, especially in *The Abyss* – was such a figure. Henri was a defective sovereign who plunged France into religious and political wars. Morally weak, debauched and unscrupulous he was also an ardent lover. He tantalized Marguerite, who saw him as a tragic figure who had not discovered his identity. She followed his life and works and, in 1929, began to draft a book about him and the religious wars of the mid 16th century. At the same time she was steeped in the poet Paul Valéry's pessimistic essay 'Crisis of the Mind'; in the wider world, the economy was teetering on the edge of catastrophe.

It was another fiction, begun in August 1927 and finished in September 1928, that was to launch her career. This one, *Alexis*, was not set in a remote idealized past. It is 'a treatise on vain desire', as the Gide-like subtitle has it and concludes with the words 'I have betrayed you'. In a sense Yourcenar had been building up to this work for a decade. It recounts the life of Alexis, a young musician born into an aristocratic, yet financially depleted, family. He and his wife Monique have been married for two years and have a son. But Monique figures as a silhouette in the background. Not even Yourcenar seems able to find words capable of expressing how Monique responds to Alexis's letter. The moral dilemma is Alexis's, who has given in to his tendencies to seek pleasure from other men and writes the long epistle that forms the heart of the novel as a reasoned explanation telling his wife why he is leaving her. Throughout he aims to distinguish between pleasure and love. He claims to love Monique but also, concurrently, needs the carnal pleasure men bring him. And he is curious about his sexual nature. His decision, he acknowledges, will brand him as a cruel nonconformist; but, though he struggles against it, he finally prefers the integrity of his inner morality and commits the drastic deed – leaves his wife and child.

I had never, even in moments of complete abandon, believed that my condition was definitive or ever lasting. In my family, I had known admirable examples of feminine tenderness. My religious ideas led me to see in marriage the only blameless and permissible ideal. I came to imagine that a very gentle, very affectionate, very serious young woman might one day teach me to love her. Except at home, I have never known similar young women.
Alexis[29]

Yourcenar was coy about the genesis of *Alexis* to the end of her life[30] but the work was autobiographical more than philosophical or scientific. When Alexis claims that 'As a child, I yearned for glory', he speaks also for Marguerite, who was never to shed this dream of greatness. The story has its roots in a particular episode in Marguerite's life. Michel and the child Marguerite had met an aristocratic but also hard-up Dutch family, the Vietinghoffs, on the Scheveningen coast during summer holidays. They kept in touch, Michel eventually having an affair in Paris with the wife, Jeanne de Vietinghoff. Jeanne was a cultured and sensitive woman, perhaps only too susceptible to Michel's advances given her husband Conrad's lack of interest in her. Their son Egon became Marguerite's friend after the two children met on the beach. (The little boy kisses three-year-old Marguerite's hand in an extant photograph.) In time she came to see the double bind of father and son: Conrad was unable to seek pleasure from his wife; Egon doted on her but she had no sexual interest in him. There was another twist too. Marguerite's mother Fernande, who died only a few days after her birth, had known Jeanne as an adolescent at a convent school. That they may have had a sexual union as girls only became apparent to Yourcenar over many years, not entirely by the time of composition of *Alexis*. In 1927–28 she was imagining Alexis's predicament was primarily Conrad's. It was a dilemma that led her to the riddles inherent in her own situation.

Alexis's literary origins are less cloudy. During the year in England with Michel (1914–15) she had heard much about Oscar Wilde. She had been reading some of his works in English in 1925 and would write a short article about him published in 1929. His famous letter from Reading Gaol – *De Profundis* – was also a moral explication, to Bosie, of the differences between homosexual love and pleasure. She also pored over the intimate journals of Gide and Rilke, two figures who had much to say about the spiritual dimension of love, even if their moral predicaments were not the same. But her style was different: as the critics said, much icier.

The reception of *Alexis* after publication in November 1929 was varied. A number of Paris publishers had rejected it on the grounds that its subject matter was shocking. Several reviewers echoed the charge or damned the novel with faint praise, claiming, in a typically French expression, that it was hardly the beginning of an oeuvre – that is, it did not have those qualities that promised a major body of work lay ahead. Other critics were amazed that a young woman had penetrated so poignantly into the recesses of Alexis's heart and head. Paul Morand, a Paris critic, was astounded 'that this is the work of a woman, who has succeeded at identifying herself with her subject so completely that Alexis truly is the confession of a man fallen victim to his penchants, so completely that there is not one line of this lucid, discreet, and thus all the more pathetic, confession that does not ring

> Oscar Wilde (1854–1900), a gifted writer and critic, had been tried in England in 1895 for sodomy. After Wilde lost his case he was confined for two years' hard labour in Reading Gaol, where he wrote a long philosophical epistle to his beloved Bosie, called *De Profundis*. The legal proceedings and the publicity attending them touched a nerve of homophobic anxiety around the world in an unprecedented way. The fallout also initiated a new era of popular curiosity about sexual difference and variation from heterosexual norms.

admirably true.'[31] Yourcenar grasped the implication of this phrase and was to continue in this remarkable identification for six more decades. She took her lead from Flaubert, the great French master of the novel who had been in the composition of *Madame Bovary* both man and woman, lover and mistress at the same time.

This was no modern lesbian coming-out but the launching of a literary career. *Alexis*, her first real book, was published and had been widely reviewed for a novice. Her biography of Pindar was being revised and making the rounds of publishers. She was writing periodical reviews and comments in the press; even a small piece about Oscar Wilde himself.[32] But she would have no part in the new manner of writing then developing and called 'modern'. More crucially, she had already discovered all the themes she would explore over the next 60 years. What remained was to find out who she was.

Marguerite knew she had been moulded as a classicist: an artist who reveres the Ancients for their achievements. She could have explained why there were no greater poets than Aeschylus and Pindar, no greater playwrights than Sophocles and Euripides, no historians more consummate than Herodotus and Thucydides, even if she lacked a university education. After digesting much of this art and wisdom, she made a conscious decision that some funda-

> Edmond Jaloux, the highly influential right-wing critic of *Les Nouvelles Littéraires*, was one of the earliest reviewers of *Alexis*. He noticed Rilke's influence, as well as Yourcenar's unusual ability: 'The revelation of a great new talent . . . She prefers an abstract style – which is the authentic French style, that of the highest tradition . . . What is particularly fine . . . is the timbre of the style and, I would almost go so far as to say, of the voice. The voice is low and deep, and soft of modulation; it is tender and harsh at the same time, descending to the depths of conscience and stirring feelings in us that only great writers have so thoroughly aroused, making itself heard, amid the din of contemporary literature'.[33]

34 LAUNCHING OF A LITERARY CAREER

mental part of her life would be devoted to the understanding, and imitation, of these giants. Though Alexis is a contemporary character, Marguerite was able to talk through him about great moral conflicts with a seriousness that put her in the tradition of the classical authors she so admired. An important critic of her day, Edmond Jaloux, identified the voice of that persona as one of her hallmarks. Yourcenar would spend many years perfecting her technique in the presentation of that voice. It was perhaps easier to capture the young man Alexis's timbre than it would be to depict the full range of Emperor Hadrian's. For now she had made an imperfect start, in a book about the most difficult of all subjects for her – eroticism.

Seductress and Traveller: 1929–1939

A writer thinks he's talking about many things, but what he
leaves behind, if he's lucky, is an image of himself.
>   Jorge Luis Borges, *Collected Essays*[34]

A lingering image of herself was already one of Marguerite's main goals. She had enjoyed life in 1920s Paris: as beloved daughter, scrupulous reader, devoted writer, and *flâneuse*. But time had marched on: she was approaching the far side of her 20s and was ready for something different.

On 12 January 1929, Michel who had been in poor health in Lausanne, died reading a manuscript copy of *Alexis*. Her father, her closest biological relation, had always been so much more than her father. He had shaped her mind for most of her 26 years before his death, yet expressed little human warmth. He had formed her as a cerebral creature rather than a sentimental or affectionate young woman. Books had not created a make-believe world in whose romantic forests she could conceal herself; but they had substituted, to a considerable degree, for the lack of parental human nourishment, as well as piquing her curiosity about the eternal realities of the human condition.

Marguerite was curious about who she really was and, in the changing political mood of Europe after 1929, curious about the future. Carefree days on Paris boulevards were becoming gloomy nights listening to frequent tales of looming economic morass. Money was not yet a problem for her personally. Michel had left her a very small legacy, which she saved, and she still had her mother's small trust fund, which would last a few years. But she lacked the wide knowledge of places and people that could confer

Photograph of André Gide c.1930

maturity on her writing. She wanted to open her eyes, glimpse the universal realities that lay beyond the provincial. Before 1929 she had read and imitated Gide and read about his exotic travels. If she followed in his footsteps, she mused, she might acquire the wisdom she was lacking. Her frequent trips to Italy had opened new vistas: the more she went the more she craved to return.

While *Alexis* remained unfinished throughout 1928, it had temporarily kept her in one place, as had the existence of an ailing father in Lausanne. After his death in January 1929 she had no major writing project underway: her study of Pindar was finished; she was struggling with a new novel about 'the new Eurydice', the story of a young Orpheus-type in search of a woman he thought he had once loved. She wrote primarily outside Paris in the small establishments that were to become her home for this decade. Being on the road, with no permanent address, suited her. But the book was not a success. The plot is defective and, though Marguerite published it later, she considered it *a complete blunder*.[35] Even in this work based somewhat on biographical experience – Michel had apparently courted such a Eurydice and Marguerite tried to learn everything she could about her – she altered the gender, transforming herself into the fictional male.

Marguerite had found a few voices, primarily by imitating

Gide, but other than in the first-person *Alexis* nothing seemed to be entirely her own. The biography of Pindar, finally published in 1932 by Grasset, pleased neither its author nor its first reviewers. Marguerite had hoped to shed light on the poet in relation to ancient Greek religion, but she was insufficiently versed in scholarship, which had made great strides since 1900, and Pindar was

André Gide (1869–1951) was a prolific French writer who wrote in all the literary forms and eventually won a Nobel Prize for Literature. His style was classical and majestic. Feeling trapped by his crippling Protestant milieu, he broke away from France in his mid-20s and visited North Africa. There he stayed for several years (1893–97), often returning, writing diaries and travel books, and tasting the exoticism and sexual freedom he sorely missed at home. He met Oscar Wilde in Algeria in 1895, an experience that changed his life. Wilde encouraged him to taste the scent of Arab sensuality, and indulge his homosexuality. From this point forward Gide's writing became more expansive as he presented the rebel's cause in works such as *The Immoralist* (1902) and *Pastoral Symphony* (1919). The hedonist speaks out in *If It Die* (1926). *Corydon* (1924), an essay, was the most daring apology for homosexuality since Oscar Wilde's *De Profundis*, claiming it was both natural and socially useful, hence placing personal experience in the service of society. For these views Gide became known, disparagingly, as an egotist. In his works he allowed problematic figures to speak in their own voices in a studiedly simple narrative – the *récit* – told from the point of view of the main character. Gide also returned to the ancient past to write about its mythic and historical figures, especially Theseus, Oedipus, and the biblical Saul. Yourcenar read much of his work during the 1920s, leading up to the publication of *Alexis*, where she went to great lengths to deny his influence. Yet there too she imitated his *récit* having read and studied his *Treatise of Vain Desire* (1925) which echoes the subtitle of *Alexis, or a Treatise of Vain Combat*. His works included *Voyage to the Congo* (1927) and *Return to Chad* (1928), the result of his sojourn among the natives in the French Congo.

the least accessible of the classical poets to anyone other than a professional classicist. What Yourcenar wrote seemed packaged and hackneyed, even the concluding sentence: *The only lesson we can learn from this life, so distant from our own, is that glory after all is nothing more than a temporary concession.*[36] The stoic pessimism she later cultivated in *Memoirs of Hadrian* and *The Abyss* had already surfaced here. But her presentation of what she called *Pindar's sensualism*, no matter how religious or ritualistic, is less persuasive than her gloomy assessment of the possibility of redemption.

Perhaps this dissatisfaction prompted her quickly to move on to something different. She cobbled together material for *A Coin in Nine Hands* from her various trips to Italy and perhaps, in part, from the new anti-Semitism evident in Paris in 1932–33. Her main story is set in 1933 (the 11th year of the Fascist dictatorship in Italy) around an anti-Fascist plot to assassinate Mussolini. Its action takes place in Rome and is unified by a ten-lira coin, which passes to each of the primarily symbolic characters of a secondary set of stories. Yourcenar herself explained what an impression on her largely apolitical mind Fascist Rome had made on her in the 1920s. She captured some of its contradictions and paradoxes, especially the resistance of ordinary Italians to this now dominant party, in the fabric of her book.

Yourcenar wrote the book on the road, the condition of impermanence that was becoming the norm rather than the exception for her. She was travelling regularly throughout Europe, especially Austria, Switzerland and her favourite Italy. Her imagination soared when in the proximity of the Alps: from the high crags of the Alto Adige area, which Hadrian visited, northwards to the Ratisbon (Regensburg) of Zeno, via the Po Valley, Rhaetian Alps and South Tyrol, over the descending plain into Innsbruck (as in the 'Conversation in Innsbruck' section in *The Abyss*) and from here across the mysterious south German alpine villages to monasteries tucked into mountain crevasses and invisible caverns.

She wrote for part of each day, sought out people and sights the other half. Sometimes luck brought her into contact with others who, like her, lived by their wits and imagination, as on the occasion when she met Austrian philosopher Rudolf Kassner (1873–1959) in Vienna, another advocate of travel.

Her returns to Paris were punctuated by late nights, red-light districts, and debauchery in what she herself referred to as her *period of dissipation*.[37] Her movements are difficult to plot. Was she in Paris, for example, in the spring of 1930 when Radclyffe Hall's pioneering and controversial portrayal of a lesbian relationship in *The Well of Loneliness* was the talk of the town? She always based herself near the Hotel de Ville in the heart of the city. In those years lesbian women met partners in a few designated teahouses, the female equivalent of the Edwardian gentlemanly clubs for homosexual men. Marguerite frequented the notorious tea salon in the Hôtel Wagram located at 208 rue de Rivoli, and other nearby spots where fancy-dress balls occurred almost daily and 'available women' congregated. She had no fixed address but drifted where chance took her. The words she wrote many years later to describe Zeno in *The Abyss* applied to her as well during this period: *Who would be so besotted as to die without having made at least the round of this, his prison?*

During these listless years – 1931–36 – she discovered Greece for the first time. Michel never took her there but her imagination had craved to see it. When the chance arose it was not to be a solitary voyage out but one so imbued with the presence of two men – both named André – that Marguerite would never be able to separate the country from their lingering memory. André Fraigneau was a young homosexual writer and editor at Bernard Grasset's publishing house in Paris. He had admired Yourcenar's *Alexis* and had rescued Yourcenar's manuscript on Pindar from Grasset's 'rejection file', thereby becoming Yourcenar's friend and her publisher for the rest of the 1930s. When Fraigneau invited

Marguerite to travel with him to Greece, she jumped at the opportunity, and soon made it a base for herself, again without a fixed address, as Paris had been.

In Greece Fraigneau introduced Yourcenar to the other André: André Embiricos (1901–75), a handsome writer and aspiring psychoanalyst, the cultured, soft-spoken, millionaire son of a shipping magnate who had by then established himself as a left-wing communist espousing political and sexual freedom. Embiricos spoke no English and conversed in French with Marguerite. Embiricos and Yourcenar took to each other, probably more out of mutual admiration and the fascination of difference, than for romantic reasons. She must have found him exotic; he, in turn, intuited her bisexuality and was intrigued by it. Later on he became obsessed with, in psychoanalytic terms, Marguerite's phallic fantasy-life. Perhaps he already saw its traces in her. In any case, the three spent charged days together in Greece during those years – 1935–37 – travelling widely in its hinterland on the Mediterranean and the Aegean. Fraigneau recalled later:

André Fraigneau (1907–92), writer and editor, became friends with Yourcenar after he discovered her biography of Pindar in Grasset's 'rejection file', where it had been for many months, and placed it into production for 1932 publication. But events, amorous and literary, intervened and they fell out. Yourcenar became so ill-disposed to Fraigneau that many years later she wrote him out of the official Pléiade Chronology of her life, the opportunity every Pléiade author gets to chronicle the years of their life as an inclusion in the Pléiade edition of classic authors. Nor does she mention his name in her extensive interviews with Matthieu Galey, *With Open Eyes* (1980, 1984). She terrified Fraigneau with her sexual advances and embittered him to the extent that he also wrote her out of his history: there is no mention of Yourcenar to be found anywhere in his extensive papers or literary remains. During the 1920s and 1930s André Fraigneau was also on close terms with homosexual playwright Jean Cocteau, with whom he later collaborated and whose biography he wrote.

'One might say that we lived from then on only for Greece and through Greece, for months, to the point where we lost all feeling for the present and were living in that intermediate space of the Fabulous and the Everyday described in the immortal *Gradiva* [Wilhelm Jensen's 1903 novel, which mixed classical archaeology with a man's awakening to sensual pleasure].'[38]

Yourcenar published relatively little in these years. She drafted periodicial essays about her travels and intensified her Hellenism. The three also wrote sketches based on Greek myths: Yourcenar's focused around the myth of the labyrinth, a theme she would later develop in several of her writings.[39] And she finally published *Death Drives the Cart*, her three stories, described as *in the manner of* El Greco, Rembrandt and Dürer, dealing with incest and sexuality. But we must not think that the years when a writer is not publishing or composing have been wasted. The time has been spent storing up experience that will be needed later; it is no less wasted than the long years when young wine seems to sleep in unvisited caves.

It was Fraigneau to whom Yourcenar's attentions were devoted. Her passion for him was as intense as it was undisguised. If the interview André Fraigneau gave to Josyanne Savigneau in preparation for her biography of Yourcenar can be trusted,[40] there can be no doubt what transpired. André Fraigneau had long before 1935 become aware of his own homosexuality: it was one of the reasons he was so attracted to Greece. He recognized in Marguerite a woman equally ill-suited to the conventions of heterosexuality. He had not known about these proclivities when he decided to publish her, although it was perfectly clear to him why he – a young homosexual man – had been so moved by *Alexis*. When, in Greece, he discovered what Yourcenar was really all about he became rather offended. This is how he remembered Yourcenar 50 years later, at the end of his life: 'She was the very epitome of a woman who loves women. Nonetheless, I soon realized that she dreamed of being the mistress of men who love men. And she was persistent, as in everything else.' Tenacious she may have been, but her looks – short, fat, always strangely dressed – were not about to charm the likes of Fraigneau. As he recalls somewhat disturbingly: 'Physically, I found her rather ugly . . . I understand why she succeeded in attracting women who love women, but they must surely have been the only ones to see beauty in her.'

Yourcenar tried to dedicate the book she was then assembling – a collection of nine prose poems based on characters in Greek myths, entitled *Fires* (1936) – to Fraigneau. She had been keeping an intensely intimate journal while in the heat of love with him. Now she reworked her pain into classical legends where love was always thwarted and tragic. In the end Fraigneau refused the dedication on the grounds he was her editor, so she dedicated it instead to *Hermes the messenger*, and still managed to convey that the book embraced the autobiography of what she called *an intense emotional crisis*. The nine chapter headings suggest how: *Phaedra, or Despair, Achilles, or the Lie, Sappho, or Suicide* and so on. Was she Phaedra or Sappho – heterosexual or homosexual? Yourcenar does not offer a clue but her disappointment over Fraigneau was clear enough – indeed it never left her, no matter how distracted she became by other women and other men.

Marguerite's love life was soon to become more complicated. Constantine Dimaras worked in a bookshop in Athens by day and had been reading and editing the Greek lyric poet Constantine Cavafy, whom he had come to know in Athens, by night. He – together with Embiricos – soon introduced her to Cavafy's poetry and she spent ever more time in 1935 and 1936 with Dimaras translating Cavafy, although they eventually disagreed on the essence of good translation. Dimaras remained, like Fraigneau, inaccessible to Marguerite but for different reasons – he was happily married. Lucy Kyriakos, by contrast, was willing to be admired. Kyriakos was the very beautiful wife of a cousin of Constantine Dimaras. Marguerite met her during the summer of 1935 in Athens while translating Cavafy. They shared common interests – both loved the snow of the Alps, where they would stay together for weeks – and became infatuated with each other. Marguerite continued to have an intense relation with her until the start of the war.

Against the background of all these entanglements, a more momentous encounter was about to take place. Yourcenar had just returned from London where she had gone to visit Virginia Woolf, having received a contract to translate *The Waves*. Woolf recorded the visit in her diary, shrewdly speculating that Yourcenar must

Constantine Cavafy (1863–1933) was one of modern Greece's most celebrated lyric poets. His subject matter is diverse but his best poems are short statements of erotic encounter between young men of the same bent. His young men meet and cruise each other in cafés and nightclubs, then spend the early morning hours in each other's arms – never to see each other again. Cafavy's poetry is bare, realistic and free of metaphoric rise, but nevertheless intensely lyrical and emotionally charged. Some valued him for a generalized Hellenism that idealized *all* things Greek; others, like Yourcenar, understood that he was in love with civilizations in decay, after they had reached their zeniths, especially the ancient Hellenistic and Byzantine culture he celebrated. Yourcenar was also attracted to his blend of historical memory with personal experience and his tragic view of life, expressed primarily in sensual and erotic imagery.

have been 'amorous . . . a woman with a past'. If Woolf could have seen her in the Wagram bar, she would have realized how perceptive she had been in the only meeting between the two writers. One day in February 1937 Yourcenar went to the Hotel Wagram, her favourite place in all Paris, but finding it quiet, walked over to the bar of the Saint James et d'Albany on the rue de Rivoli. Yourcenar was flirting with a man when an American woman from the Midwest interrupted them. One smile led to another and Marguerite invited her new acquaintance to see the Paris rooftops from her sequestered room. Grace Frick agreed. Within weeks they were friends who would soon be travelling throughout Europe over the course of that spring 1937. Nevertheless Marguerite continued to brood on Fraigneau and was still in love with Lucy.

Yourcenar was under contract to write *Oriental Tales* for Gallimard, having met one of their editors. These were stories derived from her reading of Eastern writers, mostly spiritual, which she had been planning for some time. Despite her unrequited love for Fraigneau – perhaps because of it – she also continued to work with his publishing house. She was under contract with Grasset to write a book about dreams, which became *Dreams and Destinies* (1938). This was a collection of some two dozen of her own dreams with her analyses of them, excluding those she called purely physiological (caused by bodily derangement) and sexual (in the Freudian sense). She was interested in the way dreams foreshadow destinies, as in the ancient traditions of dream analysis. The collection was shaped by erotic magic and mysticism, an old tradition of feminist exuberance from the time of Teresa of Avila and Madame Guyon, the 17th-century French mystic who was obsessed with her own dreams.

All in all, though no major work had appeared in these years, she had not been barren. Her translation of Virginia Woolf appeared in 1937, *Oriental Tales* and *Dreams and Destinies* in 1938, and she continued to work on the Cavafy project. Meanwhile she carried on her love affair with Lucy Kyriakos, with whom she travelled to Austria and which also brought her regularly back to Greece. Her new friend Grace was for the moment somewhere down the list. She would have to wait for some of these earlier projects to be finished or people to declare themselves. Her precise movements over these years (1937–39) are difficult to chart. But it is clear that, as both a writer and a lover, Marguerite Yourcenar was taking shape. The parts of Marguerite's life had grown far more integrated than they had been when Michel died a decade earlier.

There was one major piece of unfinished business: Fraigneau. Yourcenar's way of dealing with affliction, at least until the 1980s, when she was too weak to do so, was to write herself out of it. Now, early in 1938, she began to write *Coup de Grâce*, the pun on the name of her new American friend too evident to require glossing. Its form approximates to that of *Alexis*, a *récit* in the style of Gide narrating the straightforward, if pathetic, events entirely from her male hero's point of view. The story is set in a remote Baltic province in the immediate aftermath of World War One and tells of a love triangle between three young people caught up in the throes of the Russian civil war: Erick, a Prussian fighting with the White Russians against the Bolsheviks; Conrad, his best friend from childhood to whom he is emotionally and sexually attached; and Conrad's sister Sophie, whose unrequited love for Erick becomes an unbearable burden on all the characters as the tale evolves.

Was this not Yourcenar's situation? She lived her life in a series of remote outposts (in Europe and, later, on her island in Maine) and the discovery that Fraigneau was forever unavailable shocked her system, as in the novel it does Sophie's. Erick's desire for Conrad is explicitly physical; Sophie feels the agony of unrequited love in her viscera – and in her womb. Brother and sister gradually come to occupy a similar place in Erick's sensual life, despite his recoiling from all women. Conrad is presented almost hermaphroditically, displaying *child-like innocence and the gentleness of a young girl, along with that same dare-devil courage which he used to display when, like someone moving in a trance, he would leap on the back of a bull, or a surging wave.* Sophie, aware of the battle of love she is losing, flirts with Erick, trying to seduce him when all else has failed: *alone with me she unconsciously sought such occasions as amount to rape on the part of women.* Erick's response is ever more cruel: *It was on one of those occasions that I was brutal enough to tell Sophie that if I had wanted a woman she was the last I should have sought.* In response Sophie takes lovers so that Erick should think she is seductive. Erick now taunts her more than earlier: *Street walkers should hardly take over the policing of public morals*, a verbal assault that prompts her to spit in Erick's face. The rest is dénouement: Conrad is slain in warfare and then Sophie is about to be executed on a trumped-up charge of treason, at which point Erick begins to think how much brother and sister resembled each other. The day of execution arrives; Erick could have exonerated Sophie but instead he forms part of her firing squad and, at her request, shoots her twice in the face. As he does so Erick is aware of the ultimate irony: Sophie's revenge. By requesting that he alone execute her, she has marked him out for life *as a prey to remorse.* No wonder his last words are these: *One is always trapped, somehow, in dealings with women.* The story is remarkably punishing and might well be judged fiercely misogynistic if written by a man. Here, in 1929, half a century before Yourcenar became famous, *Coup de Grâce* already bears the characteristics that were to become associated with her writing. These included a terrifying doubt about members of the opposite sex and the sense that gender is the deathtrap from which it is impossible to extricate oneself except through flight.

Perhaps this was Yourcenar's verdict on a decade of romantic

Grace Frick at the beginning of her relationship with Yourcenar in 1936

entanglements. She was now to begin a new phase of life. Her nomadism had been quenched temporarily by a decade's wandering. It was 1939 and war was breaking out. Germany declared war on France on 3 September, just as Marguerite returned from the Swiss Alps. Marguerite was penniless, alone and without work: what future could she have? It made sense to accept Grace's invitation to spend the winter with her in her Manhattan apartment at 448 Riverside Drive, close to Columbia University, where Grace would teach at the women's unit, Barnard College. They sailed from Bordeaux in October 1939, just before the Atlantic became too dangerous to cross, entering New York Harbour on the morning of New Year's Day 1940.

America, America: 1940–1951

America, America, oh to be in America.
Christopher Isherwood, Sally Bowles' cabaret song in *Goodbye to Berlin*[41]

Josyanne Savigneau, Yourcenar's official biographer, has called the 1940s her dark years.[42] In many ways they were but eventually they served a useful purpose: it is unthinkable that Marguerite could have become the writer she did if she had not migrated to America. The reasons why gradually clarified themselves as the decade evolved. Now, in 1940, it is Marguerite's sense of being lost in the wilderness, without clear purpose or direction, that must be explored.

For one thing Yourcenar was not writing, or even taking notes, and would not for a long time. She had set the pattern of her creative life in the formative 1930s, alternating periods of drafting and revising with weeks of carefree abandonment and hedonism on some small Aegean island or alpine crag. Now with Grace, just a few blocks from Columbia University, in a small, dingy flat from which you could not even see the mighty adjoining Hudson River and its spanning bridges, nothing was familiar. Her translations of a few of Cavafy's poems, which she had so lovingly made in the 1930s, were published in January 1940; but that was work completed long before she crossed the ocean. Nothing else would be forthcoming until 1944. Even then, very little saw the light of day until the publication of the *Memoirs of Hadrian*[43] at the end of 1951.

Marguerite must have relished the parcel bringing her copy of *Mesures*, an obscure French literary journal, that winter. Cavafy and Greece had become closely linked in her memory, after long years wandering there like an Arcadian shepherdess with close friends, male and female. Now, in America, as she read in the newspapers about the daily atrocities across the ocean, the issue containing her Greek poems must have offered momentary solace. Cavafy was to remain her favourite poet. She would not publish her edition of his works with an expanded critical introduction for another 18 years. But in the interim she continued to identify with him as another outsider: nationally, intellectually and sexually. Many times she was to claim how much she would have given to meet him just once.

In the meantime the cataclysm in Europe intensified. As she learned how to manoeuvre in the maze that is metropolitan New York, Paris was occupied, De Gaulle began his broadcasts from London, Dunkirk was evacuated, the Battle of Britain raged and the French government fled to Vichy. After the Japanese attacked Pearl Harbor on 7 December 1941 it was only a matter of time – a few months – before the Americans would join the war. Her only letter to survive from this year, 1940, is a brief love note full of *tendresses de Marguerite* addressed to Lucy Kyriakos in distant Greece and written from Charleston, South Carolina, where she and Grace had gone for Easter. Marguerite never sent it. Kyriakos was already dead. She had been killed in the Greek bombardment of Janina, Turkey, that spring.

Yourcenar was a voluntary exile, uncertain about the future. Once settled with Grace into their apartment, she found herself yearning to join the émigré literati already assembled in New York, like W H Auden and Christopher Isherwood – who had arrived in New York only a few months before she did – and hundreds of other refugees who had flooded out of Europe in 1939. She had migrated to America for Grace, and to avoid further penury, not to escape the Nazis. But everything meaningful to her was across the Atlantic – including other women, other possible lovers – and the war made it impassable. Her stepmother

Christine de Crayencour, ageing and impoverished, was stranded somewhere in middle France, but Marguerite had no money to send her. In America Marguerite was unknown, almost penniless, and had no work. Grace paid for most items, which rendered the fiercely independent Marguerite more vulnerable than she could tolerate.

Yourcenar applied to her Paris contacts but the letters never arrived and nothing came of it. She picked up the odd lecture here and there courtesy of one of Frick's friends, as when Alice Parker found her a few talks to give in the autumn of 1940, but they paid poorly, or not at all. Frick in the meantime landed a job at Hartford Junior College in West Hartford, Connecticut, over 100 miles from Manhattan. She was to begin in September 1940, so she rented a small apartment there at 549 Prospect Avenue. Marguerite joined her, of course, and they remained there until April 1951, when they relocated permanently to Maine. But life there was not easy. Yourcenar, who in the 1930s had grown accustomed to Greek *xenia* – that unique hospitality the Greeks had been practising long before Hadrian came to the throne – suddenly found herself amidst stiff-collared bankers and insurance brokers in middle-class, suburban Connecticut.

In desperation she turned to Jacques Kayaloff, a Jewish New York businessman she had met in 1937 on her first trip to America. He wrote good French and spoke it. He loved artists, identified with Europeans, especially those Jewish émigrés who had fled from Hitler's grip in the late 1930s, and was willing to help out someone like Marguerite. But what could be done? An unmarried and unprepossessing woman approaching 40, almost as wide as she was high – her American passport states that she was 5 feet, 4 inches – with a large belly and massive chest, who dressed oddly and spoke inferior English. Her photograph on the frontispiece of this book, seated on a chair in Bordeaux in 1939, her luggage beside her but outside the camera's frame just before they sailed, shows how weird she must have looked. Kayaloff introduced her to some New York literati. But she dressed too eccentrically, especially for New Yorkers, and her English was still too rudimentary to permit anything but a comic or grotesque impression on them. Besides, once in Hartford, New York was too far for routine trips; its only joy for Yourcenar, it seems, were the famous paintings by Caravaggio in its museum, the baroque painter she had grown to love in her youth.

She sank further, becoming depressed and hypochondriacal (a condition that would hound her intermittently for the rest of her life, suggesting that the nostalgia that gripped her now was more acute than she could ever concede). It was only some time after autumn 1942 that she was sufficiently confident to think she might again have literary projects and began to translate African-American spirituals and lyric Greek poems. But there was one genuine positive. In the summer of 1942 they discovered what seemed to them a small, wild island off the coast of Maine – Mount Desert Island – and rented a tiny wooden bungalow there. At the end of their summer holiday they moved to another part of the island, the village of Somesville, into a little house next to a small cemetery where their ashes now reside. Yourcenar was uplifted. Something stirred in her, some principle of creativity amidst the silence of the sea. It could have been some primeval place in the Greek archipelago, jutting out into the Ionian Sea. This was an America Yourcenar could understand. For the first time since she had crossed the ocean she felt she was herself again. Grace recognized the change: she noted in her daybooks that Marguerite was again writing. It did not matter to Grace what Marguerite was writing or whether it was published. A suddenly dying spirit, a soul so far lost in the new world, had recovered itself.

In the autumn of 1942 Marguerite began to offer classes in French at Sarah Lawrence College, an expensive and progressive college for women in Westchester County, 20 miles north of Manhattan. At first the prospect seemed rosy, not least the opportunity for financial independence from Grace. But as time passed she started to realize how alien the place was to her. She never settled in, despite remaining in the school's employ until 1950, when she took a leave of absence to complete the *Memoirs of Hadrian*, returning for a few years after its publication. A most comic essay could be written about her experiences there: comic because of the range of misreadings of cultural codes by employer and employee alike. She could never integrate herself into this company of women, no matter how proficient their command of French, nor did she try; they, in turn, found her odd and left her to her own devices.

The world of academia was not in itself uncongenial to Marguerite: years later, in the 1980s, when she was enticed to give talks at Harvard University and leave them her papers, she was delighted and flattered. But by then she was a famous writer and Harvard treated her accordingly. For now, the unknown fledgling in America worked for the money, not to engage, let alone enlarge, her mind. Neither Sarah Lawrence College nor even the semi-wild state of nature on Mount Desert

Yourcenar in the kitchen of the house at Petite Plaisance, Maine July 1987

TEACHING IS NOT SUCCESSFUL   53

Island could satisfy her. She needed substantial writing projects.

The announcement of the liberation of Paris in August 1944 cheered as well as perturbed Yourcenar. If a truce was declared, she could travel again. She might even return to Europe permanently. How would she make a decision? It was one thing to go off to the Aegean or Alps in times of peace; if things failed she could return. Paris was always a rocklike base and her contacts and support were there. Now (1944–46) the stakes were much higher: to stay or not seemed a matter of life or death. No letters about the decision survive from these years and her private papers covering them remain locked up. It may well be that, after she had balanced the pros and cons, love carried the day. Perhaps she realized that there were not many Graces – of any nationality – who would devote their entire life to her. Whatever the process of decision-making actually entailed, she decided to stay. Time would prove Grace's devotion.

The war's end brought uncertainty and reflection. As the philosophy and commentary of those years demonstrate, 1946–48 was a time of widespread retooling. For Yourcenar, however, it resulted in few new ideas. She was commuting the 100 miles weekly during term from Hartford to Westchester, teaching her classes, eagerly awaiting summer each year – her favourite season – and the couple's return to Mount Desert. She published a few reviews in 1947, as well as her French translation of Henry James's *What Maisie Knew*, and a French magazine called *Le Milieu du Siècle* published the whole of her play *Electra or the Fall of the Masks*. These were hardly distinguished – the translation of James's novella is quite defective – but persuaded her she was going somewhere. The French Consulate's news that by the end of 1947 she would be an American citizen must have reinforced her decision to stay. On 2 November 1948 the documents arrived making her a card-carrying citizen.

But it was Jacques Kayaloff who really changed the tide. He

had promised her that if he ever returned to Europe after the Holocaust he would bring back the trunks she had left in Lausanne. These contained family papers, which she had assembled after Michel's death in 1929, and her notes about Antinous and Hadrian. Yourcenar had never stopped thinking about her emperor, even dreaming about him, and she had continued to read the historical sources in libraries in New York and New Haven during the 1940s when she often travelled there from Hartford. But she worked on the book only sporadically in the years from 1929 to 1949; since 1939 she had lacked the papers she had had to abandon in Switzerland with the outbreak of war.

Then, at the beginning of 1949, a surprise: the trunk filled with old papers arrived from Lausanne containing the lost manuscript of her *Memoirs of Hadrian*. Kayaloff, an angel in the form of Hermes, had kept his promise. They arrived on 24 January 1949. Yourcenar was thrilled and spent many months rereading them and reconstructing their meaning. They awakened some demon of creativity, or opened up a sluice that had been blocked. She had written nothing substantial or original throughout those war years in Hartford. Now she had a major project to work on – and a sense of purpose verging on mania and trance.[44] She wrote all through 1949: at home, while commuting, and on the train across America when she and Grace went to Santa Fe for the first time. She wrote into the early hours of the morning, almost turning herself into a nocturnal creature. She continued composing when they left for Mount Desert in June, and after she returned to Sarah Lawrence in September.

By January 1950 she had made progress but she needed more time and persuaded Grace, who was all too eager to cooperate, that she must leave Sarah Lawrence to finish the book. She gave notice that spring and again wrote furiously, so that the manuscript was virtually finished before they left for Mount Desert in June. Things had definitely taken a turn. The college's president had granted the leave. Marguerite's previously saturnine mood was thoroughly altered. She and Grace continued to be fascinated with Mount Desert, especially the little house Petite Plaisance which they had by now rented for several years. The woods around it, covering a couple of acres, provided both with a sense of ultimate peace and privacy.

The couple discussed the advantages of living in remote Maine. Here, in this backwater where the only language was English, Marguerite could be left alone with the French language. Since they had started to visit in 1942, Yourcenar had come to see that she even preferred not being in a French-speaking country, rather as Gertrude Stein delighted in Paris because it left her alone with English. Perhaps this linguistic fact, as much as the psychological explanations Marguerite and Grace hashed out, accounted for their decision to stay. In the summer of 1950 Grace became rather obsessed with buying Petite Plaisance. The purchase, with Grace's money, was concluded at the end of September. They returned to Hartford, packed up their possessions and were permanently installed by Christmas 1950.

From 1950–51, once Yourcenar and Frick had moved permanently to Maine, their lives began to develop into a Yourcenarthic image. The world wanted to think of them as two women stranded on a barren island in the Atlantic, alone with the elements, striving for survival – and eventually it did. Myths are universalized stories that tap into something profound in the unconscious. Yourcenar was fascinated by and worked with myths all her life, but she was quick to deny their validity when those myths had to do with herself: the myth that she had been a motherless French fugitive who fled Nazi Europe; that she had been victimized for her sexuality and escaped to America with her lesbian lover; and that she had removed herself to a seemingly barren island with this servile American woman from the Midwest. Her petitions for common sense and verification made little difference to the symbolic image she began to project. It was the very stuff of Sapphic myth of the same powerful type she was privately translating and annotating and of the theoretical Jungian variety she would soon be reading in preparation for *The Abyss*. The more the myth-making intensified, the more she was transformed, it seemed, into an international cultural icon.

Yourcenar was now perfectly clear about her motives for staying in America in ways impossible at the end of the war when she was agonizing over whether or not to return to Europe. Her contemporaries Auden and Isherwood had fled England for Berlin and then America to be sexually free. In England, where the practice of homosexuality in private was still outlawed until 1967, they were sexual prisoners. Yourcenar came to America for altogether different reasons. She had hardly been sexually repressed in Europe. Just the opposite: mired in unrequited love certainly but never thwarted as they were. She came to America with another woman because she had no money and that woman held out a hand. She may also have loved Grace a great deal. The distinction was paramount and clarifying itself daily to Marguerite as the decade closed. When she and Grace found their desert-island retreat, they could refashion themselves: not as a couple of Trojan women, so to speak, bitter that their homeland had been taken from them, but as artists who had opened their eyes to the realities of the human condition. Before the war, Marguerite had reasoned with herself that she was still too young to write her book on Hadrian and Antinous. She had travelled widely but seen little. America and Grace forced Marguerite to grow up: personally, economically and emotionally.

Had Marguerite not migrated to America she would not have experienced the despair that enabled her to acquire the empathy for the suffering of others every great writer needs. She emerged from her depression weakened but more appreciative of the melancholic condition of her Roman emperor. But if she had spent the 1940s in Nazi Europe rather than being reborn in America, her ingrained pessimism might have become personal and bitter rather than historical and universal. The war tinged Marguerite's pessimism with the same horrors that artists such as Max Beckmann registered but it was hewn from a different fibre. Firmly tucked away into a green corner of the Maine woods, it was almost as if the war and its brutal aftermath had passed her by. Her enduring sorrow was for those miseries that kept resurfacing in history. As her voice and her world-view became ever more entwined with Hadrian's, she turned her gaze much further back than the horrific events precipitated by the Nazis and other fascists to a more philosophical pessimism based on human nature itself, on what the Roman philosopher-poet Lucretius called the 'tears of things'. Marguerite's classicism could make more sense in the brave new world of America at mid-century than in the ravaged old world over the ocean.

Yourcenar as Hadrian: 1951–1955

I who would have given a year of my life to meet Hadrian.
(Comment frequently made by Yourcenar to friends and editors)

Eros, that god who is wisest of all.
　　Memoirs of Hadrian[45]

Marguerite and Grace sailed back to France on the SS *Mauritania* on 10 May 1951. Marguerite had been sending instalments of *Memoirs of Hadrian* to her publishers Plon from May 1950 onwards. By November 1950 they had received a more or less finished manuscript, but Marguerite still needed to secure a proper contract and, like all her contracts, that would need to be arranged in Paris. As the two women set out back to Europe, it was clear what remarkable reversals of fortune had occurred. Within the space of a few years Yourcenar had transformed herself from a depressed exile in America to a burgeoning author with a partner, house, new nationality and American citizenship.

A week later they were in Paris, reconnecting with old friends whom Yourcenar had not seen for 12 years, and talking to editors at Libraire Plon. Her friends, who by that time had become influential in the Paris publishing world, had puffed up the new book about Hadrian before Grace and Marguerite arrived. Plon were breathless to sign her up, which they did on 7 June, a day before her 48th birthday. She and Grace regaled themselves and their friends all month and then headed for the Swiss Alps, a place whose solitude and beauty retained symbolic significance for Marguerite. By September the couple was back in Paris and Yourcenar was sparring with her publisher, Georges Poupet at

RETURN TO FRANCE 59

Plon. The houses of Gallimard and Grasset entered the fracas, which lasted all autumn. But Plon prevailed and published the *Memoirs of Hadrian* in November 1951.

Copies went on sale on 5 December.[46] The book caused a sensation and was hailed as a masterpiece in the press. Some said it was the destiny of Yourcenar's life. In June 1952, she was awarded the Prix Femina Vacaresco. Her career was now secure. All spring she basked in her new glory as a hitherto unknown confidence built up. Her reward to herself – as always – was to travel. She and Grace went to France, Italy and Spain and even considered going to Morocco, just as in the days before the war. They had now been away from their 'island paradise' for a year (1951–52) and were as much exhausted as exhilarated. They spent July 1952 taking their farewells of friends old and new, editors, the press – indeed, it seems from the record, the whole Paris literary establishment. Then, prize in hand and with a trunk full of reviews and handwritten letters of congratulation, they returned to Mount Desert in August. By the next summer, 1953, they were back in Paris. Thus began a pattern the couple followed for a decade until Grace, afflicted with cancer, could no longer cross the ocean. They spent their summers and autumns on Mount Desert, made for Europe in the winter or early spring, and always returned to Maine in plenty of time to celebrate Marguerite's birthday on 8 June.

Memoirs of Hadrian takes the form of a first-person letter from Hadrian to his successor Marcus Aurelius. Hadrian had adopted Aurelius in 136 AD and educated him, thinking what a superior emperor he would make, as his own death fast approached. The time sequence opens late in 137 AD – the Emperor has just returned from a visit to his physician Hermogenes – and quickly moves to flashbacks of his life. He has been writing his autobiography, which was lost over time – one reason Yourcenar could legitimate herself to reconstruct it. The book falls into six chapters (all given Latin titles based on key ideas generated by Hadrian) each of the same length despite the illusion of difference among them. The first section (*Animula Vagula Blandula*, literally: *Little soul, little wanderer, little tempter*) opens with Hadrian's self-analysis of his character; then the book quickly flashes back in parts two and three to his early life: grandparents, parents, education, military training, relation to former emperors Trajan, Mark Antony, Titus, Domitian, early military assignments and ordeals. Hadrian's character descriptions are memorable, especially those of his benign sister Paulina, his mother-in-law, the Empress Plotina, who became his ally and lover, and his wife Sabrina, whom he married after ascending the throne at the age of 41 in 117 AD. Then follow the long years of travel throughout the empire and his vision of a *Tellus Stabilita* (*Steadfast Earth*). Nothing in Yourcenar's reconstruction rivals her evocation of the *Genius of the Pacified Earth* in the guise of a reclining youth – Antinous – submissively holding fruits and flowers,[47] and the intricate maze of description of Hadrian's first meeting with Antinous in 127 AD. This marked the beginning of *the fabulous years*. The book takes the reader onward into the *Saeculum Aureum* (*Age of Gold*), the drowning of Antinous and analyses of his death. Hadrian retreats into occult preoccupations after the loss of his beloved (his years of *Disciplina Augusta* – *Augustan Discipline*).

Roman bust of Emperor Hadrian recovered from the banks of the Thames

Yourcenar catalogues Hadrian's renewed faith in all things Greek rather than Roman, a form of nostalgia as much as informed intelligence about the differences between the two, his intensified insomnia and despair at the lack of sleep, his decision to return to Rome, build himself a villa (the Villa Adriana), and prepare yet more intensely for a successor, which he still had not done, and finally his death *of concern to me alone*.[48] By the end Hadrian so ardently craved his death that it became, according to Yourcenar's first-person narrative, *a hunger like that of love*.[49]

Yourcenar had been thinking about some version of this narrative since the 1920s. It was during that decade that she came across the two particular elements which first led her to the story of Hadrian and Antinous and which would attract and test her writing for over two decades until she was finally able to find the right form to do justice to them. One of these elements came from Gustave Flaubert, whose works the young Marguerite had already been reading by 1924, the year when she first mentions being at work on some type of book about the Roman lovers. To the end Yourcenar remained tight-lipped about her literary ties to the great French novelist, referring only to his adulterous heroine Emma Bovary but she clearly saw herself as intimately related to him. Just as she often merged herself into Hadrian, so, she believed, Flaubert depicted his sexual counterpart – his double – in Emma Bovary. She had read his letters referring to his travels in North Africa, sailing down the Nile beyond Antinopolis, which Hadrian dedicated to his beloved. She may also have read, or heard about, his musings on Breughel's painting *The Temptation of St Anthony*, in which the saint is tempted by lust. She certainly referred to the painting several times later in her life and could not resist the temptation to think that the hermit monk's predicament – caught between disciplined retreat and the pleasures of the flesh – touched on her life as well.[50]

But, more than anything else, it was a letter, undated but generally assigned to 1861, from Flaubert to Madame Roger des Genettes, known as La Sylphide, which captured Yourcenar's mind. It could only have done so in someone already steeped in classical history to a profound degree. Flaubert and Madame des Genettes were discussing how historical novelists pick grand subjects from the past for their books. Flaubert agreed with Madame Roger des Genettes that the Roman philosopher Lucretius was a great man who could not be compared with Byron who had neither Lucretius's 'seriousness, nor the sincerity of his sadness. The melancholy of the ancients,' Flaubert continued, 'seems to me more profound than that of the moderns, who all more or less imply that immortality waits beyond the "black void". For the ancients, however, this black void was the infinite itself; their dreams take shape and fade away against a background of immutable ebony. No cries, no convulsions, nothing but the fixity of a thoughtful face. Just when the gods had ceased to be, and the Christ had not yet come, there was a unique moment in history, between Cicero and Marcus Aurelius, when man stood alone.' For once, suggested Flaubert, 'some humans had been able, unaided and unflinching, to face their deaths.' The modern age, with its spiritual crises and hysteria, had lost the strength. 'Nowhere else do I find this grandeur,' Flaubert wrote.

Yourcenar seized on the creative possibilities of this passage from Flaubert for her own fictional universe. What does it mean for mankind to be abandoned by the gods, to have no spiritual home to be consoled in? The gods of the ancients had functioned as efficiently as Christ and his martyrs later would. But during this moment in the second century humanity had had to fend for itself, rely on its own ungodly resources. This solitary resilience – rational, proactive, sensual, forever attuned to the death of the individual – formed the basis of its unique version of melancholy: the same one the Renaissance artists who fascinated Yourcenar tried to capture, especially in such works as Dürer's *Melancholia*.

Gustave Flaubert (1821–80) was France's leading novelist of the generation before Yourcenar. *Madame Bovary* (1856–57) had been called the novel par excellence of the century. During Yourcenar's formative years of reading in the 1920s Flaubert's letters were being published in new collections, one of which she found and read. Yourcenar was awed by Flaubert's genius, which she considered rivalled in French literature only by Baudelaire's. She continued to insist that the substantive content of Flaubert's writing could not be separated piecemeal from his genius. She was particularly taken with the sexual ambivalence, or at least the sexual flexibility, of Flaubert's major and minor characters.

It was the melancholy Yourcenar wished to explore for the rest of her life. As she wrote, *A great part of my life was going to be spent in trying to define, and then to portray, that man existing alone and yet closely bound with all being.*[51]

Flaubert admired that absence of anxiety in the face of the void – no cries, no convulsions – represented by Lucretius; later commentators pointed to other responses, some so contradictory that they initiated new religions and philosophies. Among these was a renewed vigour to the two ancient types of love that the Athenian Greeks had played down: Eros, a sensuous physical love between two persons; Agape, a more generalized, almost dispassionate love for the things of this world. These forms of love depended for their interpretations almost exclusively on their practitioners. The new Platonic mystics, for example, insisted that erotic love was inherently mysterious and incapable of rational explanation – hence it formed the basis of their Gnosticism or deepest wisdom. The new sects of Christians, on the other hand, aimed to explain Agape in rational terms, barely resorting to magic or the occult. Both groups were preoccupied with love as a response to this sense of twilight void that so fascinated Flaubert – and now Yourcenar.

Among the many varieties of Stoicism was that of Lucretius, who stood before the void without props or supports and eschewed every form of occultism. He was a materialist atomist. His credo, summed up in his great philosophical poem *De rerum natura* (*On the nature of things*), developed three main strains. First, the belief that the whole universe consists of atoms, which randomly combine to give rise to all things in the creation. Second, the seemingly heretical view that atomism permits no role for the pagan gods, let alone a single Christian deity – hence the death of all gods, pagan *and* Christian. Lucretius concluded – the third major tenet of his thought – that mankind was left hanging in this atomistic universe without purpose. Man should therefore give himself over to pleasure, a life of Epicureanism. But, since pleasure was an insufficient justification for human existence, Lucretius saw the human condition to be tragic. Hence his often quoted 'tears of things' ('*lacrimae rerum*').

But Lucretius's restrained Stoicism was merely one variety among several. Other Stoics – some equally eloquent and then influential – were more pessimistic in the face of the death of the gods, responding with despair, bewilderment and profound gloom. In the century between Flaubert's letter of 1861 and when Yourcenar finished her *Memoirs of Hadrian* in 1951, professional classicists filled in the gaps, showing how large this range of Stoic responses had been in the second century AD; how the Stoics were influenced by the spread of Christianity; and highlighting the roles played by magic and the occult. Some went so far as to claim that the second century AD had been an Age of Saturn, wholly configured under the sign of despair and melancholy, during which mankind had felt so desperately abandoned that it resorted to all sorts of strange practices and weird beliefs to replace the gods. No single credo any longer unified late Roman society. Instead a new form of irrationalism insinuated itself into daily life and prevailed over any form of rationality.

In his masterpiece *The Greeks and the Irrational*, which appeared in the same year as the *Memoirs*, E R Dodds, then Regius Professor of Greek at Oxford University, demonstrated how strong the irrational strain had been among the classical Greeks and how long it had endured. By the twilight that concerned Flaubert, it changed its complexion and expressed itself in all sorts of magic and occultism. The second century AD had lost all coherence and become, as W H Auden characterised the modern world between the two world wars, an Age of Anxiety.[52] Conversions from Roman paganism to the new Christianity were rife; families were riven by it. Man was not merely friendless in the universe, but distraught. This was the social milieu in which Hadrian and his two successors, Lucius Verus and Marcus Aurelius, found themselves governing.

> Stoicism in its Roman second century AD version was primarily the religion of pagans. Gnosticism, in contrast, was primarily a Christian religion. It was predicated on the belief that the power of evil could be overcome by magic. The two religions, however, often intermixed and blended. Both pagans and Christians practised both. Much of the confusion of the epoch was caused by the lack of clear lines of demarcation between them.

Yourcenar was not herself a professional classicist but she was well aware of many of these developments in classical scholarship. Even before she migrated to America she was reading widely about the second century AD, though it is not entirely clear what she read. Books in French about Stoicism and Gnosticism had been written by the 1930s, books of the type found on the quay stalls of the Seine and in the Paris bookshops she visited. Then, in America, she read others – again mostly in French or German – in libraries in New York and New Haven. She perused books about the diverse forms of paganism, and books about conversion to Christianity. She read about the Stoic writers and thinkers Seneca, Epictetus (who Hadrian had consulted in his hovel retreat as an adolescent), Euphrates and Empedocles, whose Stoicism was based on principles of balance and retreat. Each of these Stoic responses to the void differed; and each eclectically integrated notions of achievement and happiness, which (in the words of his modern exponent Yourcenar) Hadrian would describe, in contrast to Epicurean hedonism, as *that narrow but clean bed whereon I have sometimes rested my thought*.[53]

Given Yourcenar's interest in this period 'between gods', Hadrian's successor Marcus Aurelius might seem to have been the more attractive subject. Less melancholic than Hadrian, sensitive but less preoccupied with his own death, it was he – not Hadrian – who left a corpus of Stoic writings, which have been read ever since. Aurelius's disastrous reign, during which Hadrian's vast empire would be invaded by barbarians, ravaged by epidemics and wasted by wars and the tumultuous conflicts between pagans and Christians would be intensified, perhaps seemed a better analogy for the post-war epoch that Auden had christened the 'Age of Anxiety'. Why then did Yourcenar choose Hadrian?

The answer lies primarily in the second of the two elements from which Yourcenar had begun the long journey towards *Memoirs of Hadrian*: Antinous and the erotic love he represented. Eroticism played no part in the life of Marcus Aurelius;

Hadrian (76–138 AD), the greatest of the late Roman emperors, succeeded Trajan and reigned for over twenty years (117–38). He ruled vigorously, travelled widely in the empire, and conducted the most extensive building campaign of any emperor. He also built villas, including the Villa Adriana, and patronized the arts. His love for Antinous is recorded in thousands of statues, including those in the city of Antinopolis. For his successor the childless Hadrian adopted both Lucius Aelius and Marcus Aurelius, but Aelius predeceased him.

WHY HADRIAN? 67

if anything his Stoicism devalued it. As great classicists were demonstrating during the time Yourcenar was researching and writing her book, and as Yourcenar herself somehow intuited without reading them, the loneliness of mankind then was abetted, rather than diminished, by Eros. To Yourcenar Hadrian was not merely a greater emperor than Aurelius, in part because he had been able to love Antinous; but the young man's love had also energized the emperor, and stimulated him to unify the empire into the Pax romana Aurelius later lost.

Yourcenar had been fascinated by Antinous long before she knew much about Hadrian. The great emperor had been one of Rome's towering figures; but it was young, innocent, emotionally fragile and melancholic, if also uniquely handsome, Antinous who first captured her imagination. There had been a resurgence of interest in Antinous in the late 19th century as the result of archaeological retrievals throughout what had been the ancient Roman world and, especially, in Egypt. Something of a cult developed, imagining him in the romantic role of the forlorn, almost Keatsian poet. Novelists and poets began anew, as they had in the Renaissance, to ponder the youth's dilemma and symbolic significance. No European country appeared to be immune to the sway Antinous commanded among educated readers: connoisseurs collected coins bearing his face and literati like Yourcenar visited the new statues being found. Adolf Hausrath's novel entitled *Antinous* (1884) was only one of several studies.

Yourcenar has left no record of how, or when, she first came upon him in her reading. But by 1926 she had purchased a photograph of the *gravely sweet* Antinous in the Archaeological Museum in Florence on one of her many Italian excursions.[54] And she had long since viewed his Villa Adriana on one of her early trips.[55] Her first literary attempt to write about Hadrian and Antinous was in fact a life of Antinous, which she started around 1924 and continued intermittently until 1928–29 when she became immersed in *Alexis*.[56] But her efforts to write about the sweet young deity were fragmented and formless. In June 1926 she submitted a draft of a book in dialogue form, entitled *Antinous*, to the Paris publisher Fasquelle. It was small wonder he quickly rejected it.[57]

Her dilemmas about the differences between the lover and beloved, unresolved in spite of her best efforts in the 1920s, added to her fascination with Hadrian and Antinous. She pondered such issues as the degree of sympathy between the two, the way the idolatrous, usually younger, beloved intuits the aspirations of the older lover and enables him to fulfil his genius, and the sense that the lover's greatest genius lies in having identified his true beloved.[58]

For many readers the fourth chapter, *Saeculum Aureum*, devoted to Antinous, is the book's most stunning section. It is Yourcenar's version of Byron's *Don Juan*, especially the second canto where the ragged and shipwrecked Don is washed up on a desolate Greek beach to be discovered by the naked and youthful Haidée. The lovers, Hadrian and Antinous, old and young, mighty and fragile, are each portrayed in thick description, their affection for the other dissected to its barest bones. Yourcenar finally resolved – after all the long years she had been wishing to do so – the mysteries of the lover and beloved, concluding that no love can be so intense, if charged, because it unites lover, parent, child, disciple into one, especially for the childless Hadrian.

No matter how extraordinary her comprehension of the mature Hadrian's love for Antinous – a combination of their unique kinship of temperament, discipleship, and erotic lust – Yourcenar excelled in depicting the younger man. Somehow she captured his attraction for the emperor, and intuited his loyalty. She left no room for doubt that his drowning was a suicide based on careful calculation: the decision to die long before he could embarrass the emperor in any way, not least by entering manhood himself and thereby becoming ineligible any longer for the emperor's caresses. Antinous's melancholic calculation was also based on his romantic dream of eternal beauty: the wish to die before youth's moment of bloom faded. In Hadrian's narrative: *In his dread of degradation, that is to say, of growing old, he must have promised himself long ago to die at the first sign of decline, or even before.*[59] Such was Antinous's gift to his monarch: his death in 130 AD wrapped in such camouflage that no blame could be affirmed in any quarter. It was to sustain Hadrian for his remaining eight years (130–38).

Figure of Antinous, Delphi, Greece

Whereas Marcus Aurelius offered the purer (and more notable) version of Stoicism, it was Hadrian who provided the more varied character. The figure of Hadrian gave Yourcenar the means to combine history and erotics. The time was ripe for an emperor whose combination of traits – heroic, organizational, visionary, erotic, mystical, and, preternaturally, melancholic – predisposed him to unify the empire and then apply the same frenzy both to his love for a beautiful young man and to the preparation for his own death. She respected Lucretius's pessimism but he was only a philosopher, not a great emperor who presided over the world. Hadrian was to become the vehicle through which to understand human character in its richest and most essential form.

During the long period of research and experimentation which led up to the writing of *Memoirs of Hadrian*, Marguerite made a decision that would colour her literary profile during her lifetime and afterwards: she decided that her protagonist could not be female. This must have been long before the arrival of the trunk or her delirious, manic applications to reading and writing in 1949–50. Even in the 1920s, when conceptualizing *Alexis*, or in the 1930s when writing *Fires*, she had pronounced that women formed inferior protagonists of literary works. Now, sometime before 1950, she decided that it was *virtually impossible to take a feminine character as a central figure, to make Plotina, for example, rather than Hadrian, the axis of my narrative.*[60] The position would in time cost her severe loss as the academic world came to repudiate her oeuvre, in part, on these grounds. But Yourcenar fearlessly charged ahead at mid-century with aspersions that cast doubt on her own ulterior motives: *Women's lives are much too limited, or else too secret. If a woman does recount her own life she is promptly reproached for being no longer truly feminine. It is already hard enough to give some element of truth to the utterances of a man.*[61]

What prejudice is this, trumpeted in the 'Reflections on the Composition' of her best-known book? Had she not read the great literary tradition in Britain from Jane Austen to George Eliot and in France from Madame de Sévigné to Georges Sand – hardly 'limited' or merely 'secretive' in any sense at all? Yet the biographer of Yourcenar's life hears a composite voice in this pronouncement: not merely Yourcenar speaking at the end of a global war which had been planned, managed and executed by men – all proof of the centrality of their lives – but the young Marguerite of the 1920s already becoming secretive herself.

Her book organized around women – Plotina, Selina, Faustina – is a fascinating speculation but it is impossible to imagine how Yourcenar might have achieved it. Female secretiveness was too close to Yourcenar's being for her to feel secure enough to anatomize it – in the Pléiade Chronology of her life where *antique melancholy* is discussed, for example. She herself coveted the secret path; cultivated it to her dying day; even insisted that her most private papers would not be opened by anyone until 2037. The mere suggestion that what was being hidden was so cruel it must not be known for half a century, was her final homage to secrecy. Greatness – the magisterial achievement she herself so coveted – was invested in men, she thought. If only she could have known when composing these words in the 1950s about *the impossibility of women as central characters in fiction* that she – a mere woman – would eventually be singled out for distinction by the highest academy in her native France. It might have changed her mind.

Some classical historians dissented from the general acclaim. One, the famous classicist Sir Ronald Syme, Oxford Professor of Ancient History and the greatest Roman historian then alive, scorned virtually everything historical in her account, including the life of the sovereign, which he considered pure fantasy. Syme carped that Yourcenar wrote in ignorance of the status of her sources; she was even unaware of the problems inherent in the *Vita Hadriana* in the *Historia Augustus*. Where would he start to correct her? Like other professional Roman historians, he detected dozens of errors: this fact, that detail, this date, that attribution. Page by page he enumerated her mistakes and begged 'the good lady' please 'to acquiesce' to historical truth and respect fact.[62] Acquiesce, that is, to the truth of empirical history.

But Syme had missed the point. Yourcenar had done her research extending over two decades; was persuaded that all the main pillars of the emperor's life were in place. The terrain was vast but she had mastered much of it: the two major ancient accounts – the *Historia Augusta* and Dio's *History of Rome* – and lesser accounts in the ancient world. But *au fond* she was a student of character, not late Roman Empire veracity. As a post-Romantic French novelist, aware that she was writing an historical novel, however grounded in sources, she still craved a coherent, persuasive emperor. She had seen him as modern as well as ancient; teased out his monumental psychological dilemmas. Not even

Freud could have exceeded her results. Three years of continuous writing had taught Yourcenar that, though she had set out to write a fiction, she was also a historian. But she had learned that the best historian is the one aware that no history can ever achieve final truth. What, anyway, could be the final truth of such psychologically subtle figures as Antinous and Hadrian? The truths of melancholy were layered like those of the onion: one peeled them, one by one, only to discover another; at the core were essences normally hidden from the historian demanding proof. The truths of melancholy were, ultimately, acts of faith.

She was persuaded he was at heart a Greek whose greatest genius was the application of Greek philosophical principles to governance and civic programmes. He had stopped the Parthian wars and effected a Pax romana; unified an empire extending from the Atlantic to the Russian steppes. Here ended the sources but Yourcenar pushed Hadrian's introspection further. She followed his melancholy laboriously, with the ardour of a Byronic biographer: claiming he was essentially a solitary dreamer, alienated from everyone in his government and household except Antinous, destined for death at 62, the self-murder he inflicted on himself as his only alternative to old age riddled with illness. (Zeno would also kill himself but for different reasons.) There was no ancient authority for these views, but Yourcenar came to believe in them nevertheless, fearless of the consequences as she transported herself into what she thought was the mind, and heart, of the great man she was portraying.

She continued to wonder – long after having finished her research over two decades and while writing and revising in the three active years (1948–50) – what drove Hadrian's melancholy, what propelled him to peaks of action and valleys of ultimate despair. Shaping this character – specifically the three or four stones, as it were, on which each individual rests – was her abiding challenge. Gradually she gathered together the basic ingredients: a self-reflective pensive nature rarely in conflict with the active emperor – as Hadrian himself claims: *I was eagle and bull, man and swan, phallus and brain all together, a Proteus who is also a Jupiter*;[63] his Greek sensibility; his erotics (early in the account Hadrian tells Mark that he had often *thought of constructing a system of human knowledge which would be based on eroticism*[64] – there is no known external historical authority for this fact); his predominantly homosexual disposition (Yourcenar was right not to vacillate between bisexual and homosexual identities – Hadrian was one of the few ancient emperors who was in our sense almost entirely homosexual); a lifelong melancholy predisposing him to hypochondria and other psychosomatic illnesses (here Yourcenar secretly and insidiously projected herself, a lifelong hypochondriac and depressive); a profound interest in the occult – the Orphic tradition, Eleusinian mysteries, magic; and a preoccupation with death from middle age.

Yourcenar ingeniously teased out the significance of five components in her Hadrian: his introspection, his secrecy, his bisexuality, his sway to magic and the miraculous after Antinous's death (as if he could have anticipated the miracles that would occur at the shrine of his beloved in Antinopolis), and his melancholic obsession with sorrow and death. These were the clues to the character enabling his achievement as the greatest of the Antonine emperors. A rare type of melancholy informed the first: the pensive temperament that finds itself reflecting on all its experiences. Hadrian's secrecy, much of it her own invention, she captured less well. In her version it appears slightly feminine, even feline: a cunning and stealthy latency rather than principles hidden for reasons of power and state. It was to become a bone of contention among the Roman historians who disputed her versions of Hadrian after the publication of her *Memoirs*. Hadrian's erotics she recreated more persuasively than any previous biographer, to the degree one wonders if her version can be improved upon.

It was his cult of death in the sixth part (*Patientia*, meaning

Patience or Suffering) that was her crowning achievement. Just as well that this part capped the book. Here Yourcenar not merely wrote brilliantly but thought originally as a philosopher of death: a thaumaturge alongside the dying sexagenarian ruler of the whole terraqueous globe. She shows us a Hadrian patiently enrolled in the laboratory of death, measuring the gap between body and soul, dreaming of his past and embracing the harbour of the future in the blessed house of the dead. *Let us try, if we can, to enter into death with open eyes.*[65] With these words Hadrian's narrative ends; Yourcenar would use the phrase *with open eyes* as the title for the series of interviews with Matthieu Galey that became the story of her life. This fitting conclusion, Hadrian in the house of the dead, ennobled the book, elevating it to a vivid metaphysical treatise on the status of death among the great. Yourcenar demonstrates how grief for Antinous turned lifelong melancholy into a religion of the afterlife for one who was neither pagan nor Christian – it was a religion Hadrian had made for himself. This climax is not merely didactic: the reader feels the pangs as the great Hadrian expires.

The writing of *Memoirs of Hadrian* was the artistic climax of Yourcenar's life so far. She was aware that the *Memoirs* differed from all her previous books by dint of the sheer research involved and sensed, with gathering exhilaration, that this book, deeper and more complex than anything she had already written, might be the work that would make her famous. The excitement of the

Roman bust of Hadrian, Uffizi Gallery, Florence

last three years of work (1947–50) was all the greater on account of the book's 30-year gestation period: no other project had preoccupied her for such a long time. She had lived with Hadrian and Antinous for so long that she could scarcely remember when they had not been in her frontal lobe. She *was* Hadrian, she thought, while writing. By her total immersion in Hadrian's mind and soul she felt as if she had ruled the empire with him, travelled the whole terraqueous earth with him, and lived his great love for Antinous as if it were her own. The composition of this book had not cheated her: nothing in her mundane life in remote coastal Maine with Grace could begin to scale these pinnacles. Life with Hadrian had been worth all the effort.

On 17 February 1955 Marguerite received a letter from Thomas Mann, in the last year of his life, a letter which meant a great deal more to her than any review. Mann wrote: 'Surely you can read German. I trust you for that. In truth, I would trust you for anything ever since the *Memoirs of Hadrian*, and since your *Elektra {sic}* still more.'[66] Mann's friend Hans Reisiger had given him a French copy of the *Memoirs of Hadrian* for Christmas 1953.[67] On 12 December Mann wrote to the novelist Claire Goll that he was reading it: 'it is the most beautiful book I have read in a long time'.[68] And he jotted in his own notebooks: 'Yourcenar is an astonishing woman'.[69] A year later, in 1954, Mann bought a copy of Yourcenar's *Electra* and began to read her play. Mann had become entranced with the scene in which Electra confronts her murderous mother, Clytemnestra. He was struck by the force of its mythical and sexual components. He was so enthused, he told her, that if he were not ailing he himself would have written an essay on this historical theme: same-sex confrontations. Yourcenar, for her part, construed the compliment as proof of her destiny. She replied to Mann on 7 May 1955 from Göteborg, Sweden, where she and Grace had gone after the long winter in

Var, France, on the way back to America. Politely she thanked him for the compliment, defended her interest in the theatre, and conceded that she knew little German; had read his works, even the copy of *Buddenbrooks* in her suitcase, in English.[70]

Never again would she doubt whether she was right about being someone important. Confidence was more than important to her productivity: it decreed whether or not she wrote. When she was poor and depressed in America, after migrating from Europe, she tried to write but nothing flowed. Change the situation and both ideas and words pour out. The smallest encouragement allowed her mind to magnify itself and sense that glory lay within her grasp. Like Hadrian, she must strive harder. She who had lived with him, had almost been Hadrian, as it were, should learn, she thought, from his wisdom. Now one imagines from afar her mood in the years after the publication of *Memoirs of Hadrian*, as the reviews poured in and the likes of Thomas Mann congratulated her.

Photograph of Thomas Mann shortly before his death, c.1950–55

In his last years [Thomas Mann] became very excited by a woman novelist. But Marguerite Yourcenar was a very Mannian writer, and her masterpiece, *Memoirs of Hadrian*, is homoerotic and male-bonded in the extreme; it required no sympathetic reach – he could have composed it himself. Paradoxically, the rarity of such an expression of admiration for a female intellectual indicates that his deepest responses continued to be inspired by men.

Anthony Heilbut, *Thomas Mann*[71]

INCREASED CONFIDENCE 77

Grace busily set about to translate the *Memoirs* into English. They were well settled on their island, the couple had bonded in what they sometimes called their 'country island', ensconced in the secure retreat from civilization they had created for themselves. They had carved out for Marguerite as much permanence someone as nomadic as she was could bear. Nothing would interrupt the new project: to make the *Memoirs of Hadrian* accessible throughout the English-speaking world no less dynamically than Hadrian had initiated his civic programmes around the eastern hemisphere. Author and translator, partners in this as in everything else they then touched, picked apart every nuance in every sentence. They worked by day and night for three years, 1952 to 1954, the best years of their conjugal life.

Yourcenar as Zeno: 1955–1979

I loved Zeno like a brother.
  (Comment often repeated by Yourcenar)

In the years composing the *Memoirs* Mount Desert had become a hive of activity, where Marguerite could coordinate research and a career on several continents, as much as a retreat where she could be alone with the French language. Grace still enjoyed good health (which would alter by 1958); Marguerite was finally assured that her stock with Paris publishers was secure. What remained to be decided was the next large project. What would it be?

First, in 1952, she cleared her desk and finished small, lingering tasks: notes she had compiled which she reworked as an essay on the composition of *Hadrian*; a return to her plays, working on a second script and a commentary on her play *Electra*; and the translation of, and commentary on, Cavafy's poems started in Greece in the mid-1930s which would not see the light of day until 1958. If she grew bored on her island (rarely) she revised old works – her perpetual placing of old wine into new bottles – as she did with *A Coin in Nine Hands* during this decade. But, oddly, it was her engagement with an essay she was writing about Thomas Mann that immediately challenged her imagination and led her to return to a short story 'In the Manner of Dürer', centred on a fictional Renaissance mystic and alchemist Zeno, which she had imagined in Paris around 1925. It was from this short story that, over the coming 15 years, her next great work, *The Abyss*, would grow.

Marguerite had read Mann's novels before leaving Paris after Michel's death in 1929 and periodically returned to them. During the 1940s while war raged and she was constantly thinking about Hadrian, she read Mann again, this time more eclectically, following his treatment of particular themes. Mann was her type of romantic writer: like her, grounded in history and the destiny of families over many generations (as in *Buddenbrooks*, 1901, first English translation 1924) and, like her, eternally vigilant to the erotic and secretive dimensions of the human condition. Earlier, when charting Hadrian's initiation into the secret rites of Eleusis, she had also been inquisitive about Mann's treatment of magic and the occult. Now, in the mid–1950s, having successfully published *Hadrian*, *Electra*, and, most recently in 1956, *The Alms of Alcippus* – she came to believe that, partly under Mann's influence, she had landed on a new theme in the human condition, something of magisterial interest to the writer of historical fiction she believed herself to be. Such a catalyst had Mann been.

Her longtime friend Jean Schlumberger, still in Paris, was the linchpin. His colleague Martin Flinker (an aspiring author) was then directing an ambitious publishing house named after the family. When it became clear that the French government wanted to honour Mann on his 80th birthday, to be celebrated in June 1955, Flinker offered to subsidize and publish the book. The project took shape under Schlumberger's generous guidance; soon the cream of Paris's academic and literary establishment had been invited to participate and contribute. Early in 1954, Schlumberger, aware of Yourcenar's interest in Mann, offered the lead essay – and therefore the most prestigious – to her. Marguerite set to work at once. The essays were collected in autumn 1954, the book published the following March.

To produce it Yourcenar reread Mann's works and assembled her copious notes, compiled over many years, to take with her for the winter of 1953–54 to Var, where she and Grace had decided to go. She configured her essay in two equal parts: first, a general estimate unpicking the reasons why Mann had already – even before his death – become a classic writer; the second offering an analysis of his magic and occultism. The latter part of this anatomy of Mann's philosophical humanism was Yourcenar's main goal. The occult had engaged the biographical Hadrian, consumed every aspect of Zeno's life, and Yourcenar also saw it permeating Mann's oeuvre. Hence she opened the second part of her essay with these words: *It would be easy to compile from Mann's writings a list of hermetic themes or incidents somewhat similar to the symbols of Goethe's* Fairy Tale *or the second part of* Faust, *or to Masonic allegories in the story of* The Magic Flute, *showing the marked influence upon his work of ancient occult tradition.*[72] She also noted the insidious, almost veiled, quality of his eroticism. The connections between Yourcenar joined Camus, Cocteau, André Malraux, Valéry Larbaud, Picasso, Pierre Boulez, Jules Romains, Jean Genet, Sartre, Roger Peyrefitte, Jean Schlumberger, the French Academy, the Minister of Culture and the President of France, in paying official tribute to Thomas Mann on his 80th birthday. The congratulatory book is entitled *Homage from France to Thomas Mann on his 80th Birthday*. It was published by Flinker in Paris in March 1955 in advance of Thomas Mann's birthday on 6 June. Mann was delighted to receive an advance copy in February. He noted at once in his diaries that he was reading the essays.[73] The homage was just in time – by 12 August 1955 he was dead.

Hadrian, the living, north German writer she was celebrating in her essay and the revisited Zeno who was forming, almost daily, in her mind, had never been clearer.

Mann, as we have seen, had already taken notice of Yourcenar. By February 1955, when he received her essay in the *Homage*, having read and admired the *Memoirs* and *Electra*, he was prepared to enjoy more of this French writer's ingrained classicism. Savour it he did, more than any of the other essays in the volume. Within days he wrote to her in Maine the famous letter of 15 February congratulating her on *Hadrian* and *Electra*: the master Nobel Prize Winner telling her that she was a great writer.

In the years after Mann's death in 1955, Yourcenar took many literary detours from the territory of *The Abyss*, not merely publishing the plays containing *Electra*, which Mann liked so much, but also a volume of poetry, *The Alms of Alcippus*, already mentioned, in 1956, her edition of Cavafy (1958), and a revision of *A Coin in Nine Hands* (1959). Other projects, equally time consuming, included long essays on Piranesi and on the French Chateau of Chenonceaux in Touraine where the pubescent Henri II had met his future wife Diane, 20 years his senior, while already married to Catherine de Medici, who would figure as a minor, if exotic, character in *The Abyss*. The Piranesi essay had been waiting to be written since Yourcenar had seen his engravings in Rome in the 1920s with her stepmother Christine. The interest in Catherine was driven by her passion for her favourite historical epoch, the mid-16th-century world of the final owner of the chateau, Henri II, and her reading of books about her Flemish origins – the same works that would feed into the historical background of *The Abyss*. She spent 1960 to 1962 gathering these essays into the volume Richard Howard would translate in the mid-80s under the title *The Dark Brain of Piranesi* – all this while continuing to work on *The Abyss*.

Her correspondence was also never to be more extensive than it was in these two decades, the 50s and 60s. No longer did she write letters merely to friends and intellectuals keeping herself abreast of post-war developments in Europe; now she also typed out masses of correspondence to her lawyers and publishers over the copyright of her books. Life in Maine, with its long winter months when there was little else to do, lent itself to that.

Well into the 1960s she wandered through historical byways. In contrast to the dogged tenacity with which she kept composing and revising *Hadrian* in the three years before its publication (1948–51), eliminating every distraction, in the 1960s she could get deflected for months at a time. But she never lost sight of the much more substantial *Abyss* on which her imagination was fixed, especially on Zeno himself. She was living with the protagonist in her new opus as intimately as she had with his Roman forbear.

Her work pattern was similar to that which she had followed with *Hadrian*: she did voluminous research, pored over books about the epoch, and wrote compendious 'Author's Notes' about how she had worked. These notes she revised, polished and usually published as 'Carnets', a bouquet of choice thoughts on the subject. She had developed the idea for these 'Carnets' while writing *Hadrian*, a habit she would retain until Grace died in 1979.

Yourcenar was no dyed-in-the-wool Hegelian committed to a Geist or spirit of the age – she continued to dispraise Descartes and celebrate Buddha – but she did believe that each epoch was shaped by a universal mentality or mindset, common to everyone then alive. In this respect she was a primitive historian of mentalities, for few historians even of her own generation would have concurred. She relied on these mentalities of the epoch when constructing her main historical protagonists: Hadrian, Zeno and his male fraternity. It was the painters of an age who best conveyed this spirit. Dürer's combination of classicism and mysticism was based on proportion and perspective; his paintings continued to dazzle her artistic imagination, and it was his world of the late Renaissance that she was now specifically revisiting. She kept photographs of Dürer's *Melancholia* (1514) and *Traumgesicht* (Dream Vision, 1525) on her writing desk.

As in *Hadrian*, she had chosen a homosexual protagonist destined to achieve greatness – however fleeting – by manipulating male power: the figure of the Renaissance philosopher-physician in the Habsburgian epoch of Emperor Charles V. In that era such a man might rival monarchs and statesmen. The transition from Hadrian to Zeno, as Yourcenar herself noted in two sets of comments on *The Abyss*, was relatively smooth.

The two books are nevertheless very different, as Marguerite pointed out in *With Open Eyes*. In the new book the action more than the main character's motives drive the telling. Hadrian was arguably Rome's greatest emperor; Zeno is a fictional invention despite Yourcenar's giving him a Piscean birthday on 24 February 1510 and a specific birthplace in the region of Bruges. Historical fiction often uses this kind of detail. *The Memoirs of Hadrian* penetrated a great man's psyche; *The Abyss* is altogether darker and more subversive, aiming to adumbrate the demonic side of the human condition, demonstrating that anyone who defies his society will be destroyed by it. Influential men rule this society but are simultaneously shown being devoured by the religious strife of the Reformation. Their rugged individualism and their fierce opposition to religious hypocrisy increase their misery.

The main characters of *The Abyss* are Zeno (fictional dates 1510–69) and his cousin Henri-Maximilian, a literate soldier of fortune. Zeno is a prodigy of learning bred in the Low Countries during the years when the Protestants there were being ruled by the Spaniards and French. Persuaded that books alone cannot teach him why human beings are so cruel to each other, he wanders the breadth of Europe and the Mediterranean, a fugitive from church authorities persecuting him for his heretical writings. He searches rather than doubts, willing to risk his life to discover the truth that lies beneath the surface of all things. His curiosity about himself is another driving force, propelling him to push forward again and again from place to place, as it had his maker, Yourcenar, during her years of wanderlust.

The book is divided into three equal parts clearly plotted by Yourcenar: Zeno's wandering life, immobile life and prison life. It opens with a compressed summary of his early years, leading straight to his departure from Bruges and his university studies for Santiago de Compostela in Spain, where he seeks an audience with the Prior of the Jacobites known throughout occult Europe for his alchemical skill. In those days alchemy offered a pathway to truth, for those who could fathom its mysterious ways. Zeno seeks to open his own eyes and see the world for what it is: a sink of heresy and hypocrisy where brave souls are burned at the stake while infidels are set free. This is the awesome reality from the Inquisition to the Reformation, a reign of black terror in the age of Galileo and the heretic Tommaso Campanella, themselves both frequently in grave trouble with the Church of Rome and imprisoned. Saints and sinners alike gyrate and levitate: the difference lies in their motives. Nothing was as it appeared to be: all was hidden beneath veils of deceit and deception. Zeno sees nothing at home in Bruges. Only distant places, compared and contrasted, will reveal the structures of reality he aims to discover. As yet he has no answers: knows nothing significant about the perennial human condition. He knows only what the superlative question is: *Who would be so besotted as to die without having made at least the round of this, his prison?*[74]

It is a question he invokes routinely during his long years of travel. Even so, his early years help him little to understand how he should mature. Having been raised in the rigid household of a conservative uncle (Henri-Juste), he breaks out of the mould of everyone's expectation, renounces his university studies and doubts the callow professors in Louvain who teach him. He is the most brilliant and learned of students in the university, but his disgust at the timorousness of his classmates and their fear of probing the unknown propels him – like Faust – to abandon his studies and make a pact with the world to experience it in other ways.

He flees Bruges in 1529 for the Iberian Peninsula and wanders through many countries, availing himself of diverse human experiences. These are the years of the Reformation – the 1530s and 40s – when Catholics and Calvinists were slitting each other's throats, beheading one another and attempting to crush their opponents' church in the holy name of faith. Zeno's Flemish mother Hilzonde herself is captured, ravished and beheaded. The plague of 1549 pollutes the land, killing off inhabitants of the Rhineland, including Zeno's half-sister Martha.

Zeno next re-encounters his Franciscan cousin Henri-Maximilian at a fictional monastery in Innsbruck and plies him with tales about the long intervening years. Henri-Maximilian has distinguished himself as a soldier, while Zeno has grown more iconoclastic. His thought – philosophical, theological and scientific – has become so daring that he lives in almost constant suspicion. His paranoia is heightened by his sexual proclivity to sodomy, which Yourcenar skirts and barely explores. It is sufficient for her to describe how he continues to yield to the temptation of young male flesh. Yet again he flees and escapes the Inquisition, each time living under an alias and sequestering himself in Europe's far-flung corners: middle Germany, coastal Poland, the Court of King Gustavus of Sweden whose court physician he becomes, as well as astrologer to the King's son Eric. Henri-Maximilian in the meantime dies outside Siena and Zeno makes for Paris, via several more aliases and detours, and the court of Catherine de Medici. But not even so powerful a monarch as she is can prevent the destruction of his latest heretical philosophical work. Distraught to discover that he is failing, Zeno decides to end his wandering life and return to his native Bruges after a 30-year absence. There he will share the house of his old friend Jean Myers. No sooner does he arrive than Myers' maid poisons her master out of carnal lust for Zeno, naively thinking that his death will pave the way for her lusty ambition.

The second section – immobile life – is punctuated by daily conversations between Zeno and his protector, the Franciscan Prior of the Cordeliers, which range over the whole course of human affairs. Even with the Prior, Zeno disguises his truest thoughts: so suspicious has he grown. Yourcenar worked hardest to perfect this middle section of her novel, displaying her truest historical and philosophical signatures. Its central chapter, under the name of the book itself – *L'oeuvre au noir*, literally 'work of darkness', loosely rendered as *The Abyss* – blends erudition with a classically spare style. No repetition is permitted, no word gratuitous. The amalgam of form and content enables her to give full voice to the hero's mentality: his quest for self-knowledge, his obsession to understand the deceptive world about him. Yourcenar demonstrates that Zeno cannot transcend his time and place. He is a creature shaped by alchemy, black magic and sorcery, as well as a wide repertoire of seemingly deviant sexualities then flourishing in late Renaissance Europe in a world where the legendary 16th-century heretic and alleged sodomite Michael Servetus, like others, was condemned to death *in absentia* by the Spanish Inquisition and then burned at the stake in 1553. (In this period the accusation of heresy was often reinforced by an accusation of sodomy.) Zeno is unique but paradoxically remains just another heretic. It was an age in which deceit was accompanied by magic: figures bewitched or bewitching, guided by planets, hitching their lusting bodies to benevolent stars. Zeno manages to combine a rational and logical mind – as a doctor he empirically interprets the body's signs – with black magic, alchemy, astrology and sodomy within the confines of the Hospice of St Cosmos in Bruges, whose enlightened physician he has become by the end of part two.

This middle section is punctuated by the appearances of a young Franciscan monk named Cyprian. Zeno employs the 18-year-old misogynist as a medical assistant. Eventually Cyprian tells his master about his nocturnal activities as a member of a secret group of *Angels* who make love to the *Fair One* and her maid *naked as they would be in Paradise*.[75] Zeno is stunned. He had imagined the treacherous practice died out in his childhood but obviously not. New fear and trembling overpower him. He is too carnally entwined with Cyprian for comfort: his old sodomitical vice again. Somehow the authorities will discover their illicit attachment. He knows that flight is his most prudent course of action but chooses to remain in Bruges on grounds that no matter where he flees he will be apprehended. This is a new strategy for Zeno: the idea of final entrapment without exit.

After debating with himself he decides that Bruges itself may offer him surest protection, even the precinct of the Hospice of St Cosmos itself. Now Yourcenar turns on all her powers of erudition, drawing on wide reading (detailed in her accompanying notes) in the heretical underbelly of the late Renaissance to produce a rich tapestry of the contradictory heroic and aberrant life of that time. Cyprian's forbidden orgies are remnants of the historical Adamites, early Christian hedonists who survived into the 16th century and about whom Yourcenar had read. Dutch and Flemish scholars had retrieved the secret history of the Adamites and she read these languages fluently. Sometimes called Brethren and Sisters of the Free Spirit, they practised nudity and advocated group copulation, dancing and fornicating nocturnally under the moonlight, as Cyprian recounts.[76]

The plot now thickens: Zeno is implicated. The *Fair One* – concubine to a dozen young men – becomes pregnant and kills her prematurely born infant; apprehended, she denounces her lover Cyprian and confesses to the judges in Bruges the nocturnal debaucheries of the naïve band of Adamites or *Angels*. Cyprian, in turn, is interrogated and to save himself he implicates others, especially his master Zeno, already suspected of sodomitical activity with the fair young monk. The authorities now turn on Zeno and his crime of sympathy for the young revellers, buttressing their arguments against him by resort to Zeno's blasphemous writings, which had been burned for impiety. Twenty-four indictments are compiled. Zeno appears before the Tribunal of Exception, defending himself rationally and scientifically but to no avail. The only escape lies in retraction and recantation: to disown all he has believed and written. He refuses to do so and a death sentence is given. Finally, unwilling to die at the stake, he chooses suicide and slashes his tibial vein and the radial artery of his left wrist with a hidden blade. Even in this final act he monitors his own reactions – anatomically, physiologically, psychologically – as the blood ebbs from his body on 17 February 1569, one week short of his 59th birthday.

Yourcenar's novel is indeed dark but it must be understood as more than a tale of nocturnal intrigue and subversion. She has analyzed a treacherous era in history no less than the most competent professional historian would. The building blocks of her case come from the major heretical figures of the period: Paracelsus, Campanella, Leonardo da Vinci, Servetus, Giordano Bruno, surgeon Ambroise Paré, anatomist Vesalius, botanist Cesalpino, Nicholas Flamel, printer Etiénne Dolet, Erasmus and other staunch seekers of truth in the Renaissance.[77] She aimed to accomplish in her own way what Marlowe and Goethe and others who have written about the Faust legend have done for their exceptional hero: an exploration of early modernity through an heroic figure – whether Faust or Zeno – caught in the unceasing quest for the accumulation of knowledge. The more Zeno learns, the more he, like Faust, wants to know; and the more he knows, the more fascinated he becomes by the lust of his body. He feels the oceanic pull of his sexuality but he cannot name it or fathom its origins. Time quickens the pace of his crazed search: every day seems to be faster than the previous. He cannot escape the shackles of ancient wisdom, especially Greek theories about time and change; nor renounce his own former writings (The *Protheories* and *Prognostications of Things to Come*) because he believes his heresy to be true. If in his life he has been a wandering atheist and negating sceptic, now he also recognizes that ultimately there can be no escape: this is why he decides to die the more painful death of suicide than attempt to flee yet again. His final surrender must be seen as personal growth rather than abandonment of truth. By dying at his own hand he has been denied immortality – for having committed the sin of self-murder – yet achieved the perfection of free will.

There are many parallels between *The Abyss* and the *Memoirs of Hadrian* but the main difference is the place of love and desire in the two books. Hadrian accomplished what he did for the Empire out of grief, in large part, for Antinous. Hadrian could not have been so fervid to build Rome to what it became under his rule without the creative drive of love. His love for Antinous had been both erotic and passionate: one without the other was unimagin-

Yourcenar and Elie Wiesel congratulate each other in Paris, 1968. After both had won Literary Awards. Yourcenar was Awarded the femina Literary Prize for her book *L'Oeuvra Au Noir (Work in the Dark)*, and Wiesel won the Medicis Award for *Mendiant De Jerusalem (A Beggar From Jerusalem)*

able. But Zeno's love affairs, with both women and men, desperately lack affect: their pitch of attachment and (what we would call) emotional enmeshment is routinely low. The emotion of love for another person may be impossible for Zeno, as it is for his protégé Cyprian. Cyprian copulates with both women and men but lacks emotional involvement with either gender; this is why the 'Angel' who bore his child loathes him. Likewise, although to a lesser extent, Zeno indulges in the mysteries of sex almost as if they were black magic experiments: something the alchemist tries but eventually renounces in his quest for the Philosopher's Stone. Sodomy is convenient for Zeno, the wanderer and fugitive in eternal flight, as is heterosexuality for the prior Henri-Maximilian; yet neither has much truck with women. And even for the other figures – Cyprian, Martha, others of the 'Angels,' and the dozens of minor characters who enact carnal love – sexual liaison is rarely accompanied by emotional attachment. It is as if Yourcenar's frescoed tapestry-world has separated itself from the emotional fever of Hadrian's.

Yet Yourcenar has not altogether abandoned her female fictional characters, not even her homosexual women. In *The Abyss* she includes, if in minor roles, powerful homosexual, or bisexual, women of the epoch who manipulate courts as well as consorts. There is Margaret of Austria, Regent of the Netherlands, who is responsible for the Treaty of Cambrai (1529), signed in the year the novel opens, representative of the female sodomy then flourishing in northern Europe. Yourcenar represents Margaret as a female equivalent of the then powerful aristocratic male sodomites. Hers is power through gender inversion rather than a physical act of penetration. Then there is the widowed lady Zeno meets in Froso in the far north of Scandinavia. More hermaphroditic than aligned to either gender, her bisexual anatomy impresses Zeno who claims that she could have been a male companion for another man.[78] Also here is the obscene and profane consort of Henri II, King of France, Catherine de Medici (1519–89), whose bisexuality was legendary in Zeno's world. It is likely that Yourcenar constructed her on the model of the ancient Greek Baubo (see sidebar), for she wrote in her notes on the book that *the obscene and secretive Catherine is a Baubo*.[79] Catherine, like Baubo, is crude, far more than her regal husband Henri II. Her sexuality is robust and masculine.

Throughout the 1950s and 1960s Yourcenar had been reading beyond the primary annals of Renaissance history. She had been profoundly moved by Karl Kerényi's archetypal study of the mystical, female rites of Eleusis. Even before reading Kerényi's book in the last stages of revision of *The Abyss* in 1965–67, she had incorporated materials about these rites in the *Memoirs of Hadrian*. She learned that Hadrian had built the triumphal Roman arches, for example, at the entrance to the Temple of Eleusis, and that the Eleusinian mysteries were enlarged in his time to encourage people from all over the earth to travel there for initiation.[80] If these crude women wielded power in the Eleusinian world, they also do in Yourcenar's Renaissance reconstruction. But now, as she finished *The Abyss*, she was armed anew, thanks to Kerényi, with the definitive reconstruction of Eleusis and its practices. Kerényi presented new material about bisexuality and suicide by fire in the ancient world, some of which Yourcenar incorporated. He explicated Agdistis, the bisexual primordial form of the great goddess present at Eleusis.[81] And he showed how the devotees of Eleusis believed in an abyss between the earth and the underworld, entered through a mysterious hole, not visible to the naked eye, at Eleusis: 'the ear of grain that had opened a vision into the abyss of the seed'.[82] Yourcenar was deeply interested in this Eleusinian version of abyss for the light it shed on her Reformation abyss. More pressingly, perhaps, Yourcenar herself was growing old, though not yet a Baubo. Can the obscene old lady Baubo, reconstructed as Catherine, have resonated personally?

Yourcenar claimed in several interviews in 1969–72 that the origins of *The Abyss* lay in old family papers she had discovered in her father's library containing such names as Hilzonde and Alberico, and in a book about Belgium in the Reformation she read at 18: J B Blaes's *Mémoires anonymes sur les troubles des Pays-Bas*. It may be so, although her memory was often faulty. Even so, her reading of contemporary material also fired up her imagination, coupled — as it was — to solitary rumination on a sequestered Atlantic island, which she had not left for over a decade. The combination produced a unique book in the annals of Western fiction. Its true sources include the Greek philosophers she had studied at the time she was writing about Hadrian, and the diverse Renaissance figures mentioned above, and such artists as Hieronymus Bosch and Dürer. She filtered some of her knowledge about ancient Stoicism directly into Zeno's character; she was influenced by those late Empire Stoic diehards who had been converts to Christianity, and who so often, like Zeno and Cyprian, vaunted their celibacy in the form of misogyny. She absorbed her sense of the fusion of alchemy and psychology in the human psyche from Jung and Kerényi, and sculpted Zeno's suicidal ending with Romanian historian Mircea Eliade's condition of *rubedo* in mind.[84] This is a psychic phase

> Károly (Karl) Kerényi (1897–1973), Hungarian archaeologist and psychologist, collaborated with Jung on studies of the major human archetypes, including sexual types under the influence of alchemy and black magic. Here, in his landmark book *Eleusis* on the re-creation of mother and daughter relations at the secret rites of Eleusis in ancient Greece he explained the rise of the obscene old woman Baubo, wife of Dysaules, who had been exhibited in the Eleusinian processions. Her profane and disgusting belly dance revolted observers and worshippers alike. Her obscene jokes were said to have moved Demeter to laughter, so much so that the goddess saved her from death at the hands of her enemies. Yourcenar underlined these passages about Baubo in her copy of Kerényi's book.[83]

alchemically associated with death and dominated by the colour red. As Zeno watches the blood flowing from his veins he blissfully regresses into the amorphous universe, just as Eliade had described, willingly integrating himself into the vast abyss of Chaos.

Yourcenar read the treatise on psychology and alchemy that C G Jung wrote jointly with Karl Kerényi and refers to it in the notes to *The Abyss*. Passages in their Epilogue may have stuck in her memory as she wove her plot: 'In a sense, the old alchemists were nearer to the central truth of the psyche than Faust when they strove to deliver the fiery spirit from the chemical elements, and treated the mystery as though it lay in the dark and silent womb of nature.' She also read and owned books by the brilliant historian of religions, Mircea Eliade (1907-89). His book *The Forge and the Crucible* (1956) was a source for the alchemy in *The Abyss*, as well as aspects of the novel's sense of man's role in the cosmos.

Zeno would seem, then, to have answered his own famous question: *Who would be so besotted as to die without having made at least the round of this, his prison?* For this Yourcenar greatly admired him: Zeno, her fictional child. Zeno's realization that one must at least make a *round* of this *prison* was at the heart of the beliefs on which Yourcenar had constructed her own life, especially its nomadic portions. Like him she had been immensely proud, often impossible. There is much autobiography in her conception of this troubled Renaissance *homo universalis*. Even so, times had changed. These were no longer the 1920s, when she – like her fictional hero – had sought to discover her identity through travel, even if the earth she was wandering in was a *prison*, or the 1950s, when the whole Western world seemed to calm down after global cataclysm. The mood of the 1960s wiped away much that had been taken for granted on both sides of the Atlantic. Yourcenar completed her book as the wave of that blazing decade in America crested, even extended its undercurrents into insular Maine.

One could affirm that *The Abyss*'s still very French author had been in America only in body, not mind. She read French, wrote only in French, spoke French at every possible moment and dreamed in French. She had never installed herself into America, nor would she. Yet it was a fact that she had produced her masterpiece in instalments over a decade (1957–67) in the northeast USA. From there it was sent to Gallimard in Paris, after a two-year battle the author had conducted with the house of Plon. Gallimard published it on 8 May 1968, just days before students stormed the Left Bank and brought Paris to a grinding halt. To great acclaim Gallimard issued 20,000 copies on the day of publication, 40,000 by July, and a huge 60,000 by year's end. For Yourcenar this was a record.

The critics – entirely French-speaking – acclaimed it a masterpiece, as they had *Hadrian*.[85] They repeated their praise of her perfection of classic style and control of form. They noted again the gendered nature of her writing: *The Abyss*, they said, was the most 'virile' of her books, even more so than *Hadrian*. Having made a case for 'virility' they teased out the implications of their claim: that Yourcenar was the most virile, or masculine, of living female writers; that in writing as a man she lacked emotional warmth and tenderness; and that both her form and content were rational and logical in just the way men had been psychologically perceived to be down through the ages. There was nothing soft or passive about the feel of the book, they said. Their main complaint was that she lacked sentiment – that the book was cold. She herself would be the first to concede that Zeno lacked affection and emotion when compared to his Greek forbear, Hadrian. Many critics found both Zeno and Hadrian hard.

She read the reviews, thrilled and puzzled. She had never seen herself as hard or cold, let alone 'virile', despite her well-known inflexible pride. Was pride masculine, she wondered?[86] Despite the accolades, *The Abyss* would never attain to the status of its predecessor, nor did it sell as many copies. How could it?

Something fundamental had changed in the world since 1951. Readers in the early 1950s, looking to Hadrian for guidance and leadership in a totalitarian world gone amok, had different needs in the late 1960s. New wars had arisen. The blazing 1960s took a toll on all sensibility: the question now, on both sides of the Atlantic, was not how one man could battle for the truth against a totalitarian regime but whether excess and liberty had gone too far. Readers wondered how man – and woman – could return to a position of social balance and cultural stability.

How could freedoms of expression and conduct combine with a sense of decorum – social, political, economic – capable of ensuring that Western civilization would continue to thrive? Persecution, especially of the type meted out to Zeno, was no longer in the centre of every reader's imagination, at least in the English-speaking world, as Vietnam, Gay Lib, and the Civil Rights Movement continued to rock America. Robert Kennedy and Martin Luther King had just been assassinated (spring 1968) when the reviews for *The Abyss* began to appear. The questions raised by the sexual and social revolutions of the 1960s were not to be answered by a book in which gender relations were so imbalanced and existential rebels like Zeno find their only escape – no exit – in suicide. Even in France the Age of Sartre had come to an end in the sit-ins on the Boulevard Saint Germain. All this took its toll on Madame Yourcenar's book, no matter how obsessed her small band of critics was with her 'virility'.

The Abyss was not read much anywhere except in France in 1968: for the simple reason that it had not yet been translated into English. It would not be translated until almost a decade later, in 1976. Still, in France it was hailed and proclaimed, and in France, and France only, Yourcenar was growing more famous every day. Hence it made a difference there how her new book stood up against the old.

Perhaps Yourcenar herself provided a clue to what must have

been at least partial disappointment when she compared her two masterpieces in a heartfelt letter to Belgian critic Michel Aubrion. *I certainly do not deny the profound difference between the two books, one that resides in that darkest of epochs in* The Abyss, *and also in the fact that Hadrian is more or less all-powerful and Zeno is obscure and persecuted, but I have a profound sense of its being a question of two stages of the same journey, and this is no doubt what explains that I could have dreamed of writing these two books at the same time around the age of twenty, without, of course, managing to do so.*[87] They may have represented two parts of the same journey to her, but they did not for others.

The resonance between her new book's title (work of darkness) and her own pattern of nocturnal composition could not have been lost either on her or on Grace. Writing into the early hours of the morning, working through the night, Marguerite must have felt on numerous occasions that she had been with Zeno in more ways than one. The books were unified by more than their philosophical content: both protagonists were obsessed with the occult and mystical, both were tempted by suicide. In some meaningful way Yourcenar had finally liberated herself from both figures by 1968 after four decades of plotting and rewriting.

In the minds of her readers more than her two protagonists were conflated. The gap between author and character had also grown smaller. Despite her subsequent protests after 1968 about the gulf that lies between herself and these figures, that space somehow seemed to have shrunk. Many readers had the lingering sense that she had cajoled herself into believing all along she was Hadrian, could now be Zeno. The sense, which had been gathering from the time of publication of *Hadrian* in 1951, that she actually believed she was Hadrian was felt and remarked upon all the more after the publication of the new book.

It was an identification she would never live down, despite further institutional glory and recognition in the next decade. Small wonder that she was now perceived to be the most 'virile' of all living female writers: not merely in France but everywhere. The feminists in America were soon to say she was not merely virile but trans-gendered and cross-dressed, engaging in narrative transvestitism: this was part of their new critical idiom. In the long run the impression may have widely proved fatal to the sense of her overall accomplishment.

Immortal Exile: 1979–1987

Talk is all that finally matters.
  (Christopher Isherwood to John Lehmann on arriving in America)[88]

The euphoria of publishing *The Abyss*, which finally enthroned her greatness, and then finding it so well reviewed, lingered into 1969. Marguerite and Grace travelled to Europe in the autumn of 1968. When they returned to Mount Desert in the spring of 1969 several American colleges awarded her honorary doctorates. Her publishers Gallimard (now that Plon had finally been eliminated) gave her carte blanche. The Belgian Academy sounded her out, in 1970, about election. The French would follow suit by decorating her with the Légion d'Honneur. She was invited to lecture and make presentations on both sides of the Atlantic.

But dark clouds were gathering, domestically and creatively. Ever since the late 1950s her love for Grace had been altering, or perhaps more accurately faltering; not diminishing but changing its habit and hue and this at least gave her pause. It was not their differences that could no longer be reconciled – for example that Grace adored children and constantly gave them parties while Yourcenar eschewed their company and felt threatened – ultimately it was the nature of their bond in the first place, and the type of control each wielded, which was putting the union they had made in the 1940s under pressure.

Josyanne Savigneau has taken great trouble in her biography to chronicle these alterations and explain them. There is no need to repeat her subtle analyses except to note that much of the speculation is idle: Yourcenar's private papers from the years 1935 to 1945 – the first decade of her life with Grace – are sealed until

2037. Until they are read it is premature to speculate about her conjugality with Grace or seek reasons for its transformations in the light of how the pair originally bound themselves together. The other, more urgent, matter is that the two women, both born in 1903, were growing old: the French woman was declining but still vitally creative and ready for life's next challenge; the American much less pliant and no longer nomadic as she was slowly dying. Love, whether for the same sex or another, changes its hues in old age. Decrepitude is no catalyst to intimacy, especially when one's chest has been burned up in radiation.

Grace's health was now markedly unpredictable. She was translating *The Abyss* (1970–76). Her breast cancer, diagnosed in 1958, had returned in early 1969. Marguerite also had to have an operation and wondered if she too had breast cancer. The outlook was sufficiently good in 1969–70 for Grace to accompany Marguerite to Belgium early in 1971 for her election to the Académie Royale in Brussels in March. They travelled widely, going to Spain in Holy Week, and to Zeno's Bruges in April. While in Belgium members of the Crayencour family sought her out, suddenly aware that this estranged relation who had run away to America with another woman, and who had lived so long on the other side of the world, was now an international star. Yourcenar spent most of May in Paris among the literati. But after the two women returned in July 1971, Grace collapsed and was placed in the Bar Harbor Hospital on their island. The trip they had just taken to Europe would be her last. For the next decade Yourcenar would remain on the island out of deference to her relationship with Grace. It was an endurance she never forgot.

While Grace was genuinely ailing, Yourcenar now, astonishingly, seemed to be imitating her. Marguerite developed mysterious ailments, fevers and nausea, and had herself diagnosed and treated in the Bar Harbor Hospital in October 1972 for over a month. She started to keep a *health journal*. The more puzzled the doctors were, the more selfish she grew: she took to lamenting her mortality and fixing on eternity, as she would in *What? Eternity*, the third volume of her memoirs, published after her death in 1987. Just as Grace needed her most, Marguerite was suddenly unavailable. But she rallied: the fever receded, germs disappeared and she again felt strong. Grace continued to organize 'Madame's' life, keeping the daily records and notebooks, filing papers and answering correspondence. Poor Grace would never extricate herself from the malignant cancer eating her up. As the photographs show, she was wasting away.

Marguerite had learned before to bury herself in work when her nomadic penchant came under stress. She did the same now. As she grew increasingly aware that travel was out of the question, she turned, once again, to old writings requiring completion or revision and, of course, to her vast correspondence. Now, in the years around her centenary, we view Yourcenar as an historical novelist above all. She is not usually seen as a major figure in the

Yourcenar photographed in front of Petite Plaisance, Northeast Harbor, Maine

history of letter-writing in the way her models, Gide and Mann, are. Yet she wrote a vast correspondence that is sufficiently rich to be studied in itself. It sits in state, as it were, hundreds of pages thick, constituting one of the important 20th-century statements about Anglo-French relations.

Part of her correspondence was her endless battles with her publishers. In 1969 to 1970 as the doctors watched over Grace, Marguerite returned to spar yet again with Libraire Plon, who still retained the copyright of her earlier novels. She also went back to her plays, revising and editing them for publication as a collection of her theatre works. She must have known her plays were among her least successful literary compositions, rarely to be mounted, but she never lost faith in their value to readers. She also finished an essay about the fragments of Empedocles, the ancient Greek pre-Socratic philosopher whose vision of eternal strife as the basis of the human condition moved her. And she finished her translation of Hortense Flexner's (pen name for Hortense King) poems, which Gallimard gladly published as they would anything Yourcenar sent them now, to which she prefaced a critical introduction. Flexner was a young American woman of limited literary ability who lived on a neighbouring island, Sutton. She frequently visited the couple on Mount Desert, took photographs and went riding with them, and eventually persuaded Yourcenar to translate her poems. Yourcenar, for her part, was fascinated with this young woman, so different from herself, yet whose imagination she tried to fathom. These were not major preoccupations, but they kept Marguerite busy. And if she grew genuinely bored, which she sometimes did, she could always initiate new proceedings against the likes of Libraire Plon, which she did at the start of 1970 for their imperfect reissues of *Alexis* and *A Coin in Nine Hands*: she claimed they were *riddled with errors*.

While Grace bore her terminal illness with dignity, Marguerite relied on her interior space and reverie. She herself, she thought, was not so far from Zeno and Hadrian: she was still consumed, like the first, by wanderlust, and like the second, the great Emperor, still craved further glory and greatness. Yet she did not stir. She neither returned to Europe nor put herself up for the small lecture tours she had previously enjoyed with Grace in America. She stopped horse riding, which she had turned to late in life.

In 1972 to 1973 she published nothing. What was she doing? The awards were accumulating, for one thing. The city of Monaco awarded her their literary prize; honorary degrees from American universities also continued to accumulate (Colby College followed Bowdoin of a few years ago). It would be interesting to speculate whether these awards from local universities in Maine encouraged her to become assimilated after more than 20 years. She wrote almost a dozen essays ranging from classical topics to modern ones, a habit she had developed during her years of travel in the 1930s. These included a substantial appreciation of André Gide, which she expanded from a talk given at Smith College in Massachusetts (the college had given her an honorary doctorate in 1961), and a new appraisal of Virginia Woolf.[89] Here Yourcenar called Woolf timid and sparkling, found defects everywhere – not surprisingly, as the two women had not got on. She was publishing in minor magazines and journals, not having entered the mainstream of American academia, although she had always felt comfortable with academics of all nationalities.

The awards, including the Grand Prix National des Lettres from the French Ministry of Culture, continued to roll in through 1974. Nor had Yourcenar been idle. For several years she had been drafting a set of memoirs about her family whose main theme was fate or, in the Greek she adapted to her title, Ananke. These volumes, like the early *Alexis*, were meant to recount her personal awakening to the reality of her past. They were not conventional memoirs, but instead blended genealogy, history, the biography of unknown figures, and local customs in Flemish France. Here she could demonstrate that she was a proper Crayencour, despite being childless. Her books – her life's work – wrote her into history and served to validate her place at the crown of the Crayencour dynasty.

Even by 1974 the conception of this autobiographical trilogy swelled to immense proportions as she struggled to contain its scope while focusing on colourful characters like her cousins Octave and Rémo; the latter an ideologue who shot himself in front of a mirror to watch himself die. She called the trilogy *The Labyrinth of the World*, adding a subtitle to each: *Souvenirs pieux* (the French phrase on condolence cards sent out when someone dies) to the first (1974), *Archives du Nord* to the second (1977), *Quoi? L'Eternité* to the third (1988), the first two being translated after her death as *Dear Departed* (1991) and *How Many Years* (1995). Volume three (subtitle literally translated as *What? Eternity*) was never finished and has never been translated into English. She lifted her title – *The Labyrinth of the World* – from the 17th-century Czech philosopher Comenius (1592–1670), some of whose works her father Michel had translated from English into French and read to her during her adolescence. Comenius's satirical tone about the labyrinth of human ties, which later became the basis for his utilitarian philosophy of education, made an impression on her. She eventually saw her own ancestral Flemish world, from the Renaissance forward, in these striking terms: teasing out of the maze family secrets and awkward personalities.

Yourcenar's unfinished trilogy, the product of her last decade of writing, totals over 1,000 pages. It takes in more than Comenius's acerbic view of human life. Her dominant metaphor of the labyrinth was adopted from classical mythology where the Minotaur, monstrous offspring of Pasiphae and a bull, had wreaked havoc on the court of the gods. With the head of a bull and body of a man, he was eternally deceiving; Minos, husband of

Pasiphae, thought the Minotaur so destructive that he commissioned Daedalus to build a labyrinth to contain the monster. Yourcenar had been fascinated by his image since the early 1930s, when in love with André Fraigneau whose favourite mythological figure the monster was. During her dark years in Hartford in the mid-1940s she even wrote a play about the Minotaur called *To Each his Minotaur*, one of her most nostalgic acts during that decade. Now, near the end of her life when surveying her roots, the image of the labyrinth again became supremely important. A labyrinth conceals and contains monsters or monstrous things. As Yourcenar grew older she came to think that, symbolically, the labyrinth concealed, most of all, the human unconscious and its thoughts. Marguerite wanted to hide her unconscious thoughts from the world: the labyrinth was the perfect place to conceal them.

> *I borrowed the title from a very great but little known work,* The Labyrinth of the World *by the great seventeenth-century Czech writer Comenius . . . Comenius's book is a very beautiful one, differing by its bitterly satirical tone from its near contemporary, John Bunyan's celebrated* Pilgrim's Progress, *to which it is related by genre. I've always been astonished that lovers of 'world literature' have not discovered this book, which is to writing approximately what Bosch and Brueghel are to painting.*
>
> Yourcenar, commenting on the title of her trilogy[90]

Yourcenar ploughed on despite Grace's recurring bouts of illness. She could not imagine life without a project; her path to glory would turn into a dead end. Besides, Grace was determined to finish her translation of *The Abyss*, which she could pursue only intermittently given her condition. Grace alone would be the first translator of both magnum opuses: the lover's tribute to the 'Madame' (as she still referred to Marguerite when talking to others) in whose intellectual temple she worshipped. The awards and decorations continued to arrive, partial recompense to Yourcenar for her new geographical immobility. The Grand Prix

National des Lettres awarded to her in 1974 had led to further requests for articles or reviews – anything she could supply – in *Le Figaro*, *Le Monde* and other leading Paris newspapers. Her name was already a household word.

Grace finished her translation of *The Abyss* in 1976. It had taken her a decade (1967–76). Three years later she would be dead. Yourcenar's American publishers had entreated her to find another translator, telling her that unless the book appeared soon in English it would be forever written off. Yourcenar categorically refused: while Grace was alive she permitted no one else to translate her work – not even a short article or review. This was her unflinching devotion to the woman with whom she had shared her life, and bed, no matter how tempestuous their relations had been over four decades. One can only imagine Grace's joy in that summer of 1976 when the first copy arrived in the morning post. She had lived to translate both her partner's masterpieces. Now the rest, she knew, was decline.

In Grace's remaining years she did her best to continue doing what she had done since 1939, when they went for the first time together to America. She received their largely French guests with poise and even thought she might live long enough to translate the first volume of Marguerite's new trilogy, *The Labyrinth of the World*. When film-makers arrived on the island seeking to persuade 'Madame' that she should allow cinematic adaptations, it was still Grace who orientated them. In 1977, it was Grace who announced to Marguerite, after opening the post, that the Grand Prix of the Académie Française had been awarded to her on the publication of the second volume of *The Labyrinth of the World*. Still more momentously, it was Grace who, in 1978 apprised her that the Académie Française was considering her elevation to the status of an 'Immortal', the first woman to be nominated.

Yourcenar's ideas continued to percolate. In 1977 she published an essay on Dürer's mystical dream (*Traumgesicht*, 1525), a companion essay to its two predecessors on El Greco and Rembrandt. She was still rewriting in the way she had 50 years ago as a young woman. Her essay triggered letters and debate; she followed it up with yet another essay on Dürer's influence on the post-Renaissance world.

Among the journalists and cameramen who came to visit was Jerry Wilson from Arkansas, a terrifically handsome 28-year-old, who spoke good French with a southern drawl. He arrived at Petite Plaisance in 1978 with a French television crew filming her as she read from the new volume of memoirs. Maurice Dumay, the team leader, was his boyfriend. Grace liked him at once, as the daybook records; but little did either Grace or Jerry know at that time that his future fate would be with 'Madame', who was stricken with attraction to this young man of another generation. This was the Yourcenar who was forever aiming to be intimate with – and thereby possess – the young Hadrian or Zeno.

While Grace deteriorated, Marguerite grew strangely productive, as if she could carry on for another half century. Her imagination was as fecund as ever; the words came. She worked away on her new book, a collection of three stories collectively entitled 'An Obscure Man', all three pieces deriving from the stories Yourcenar had written in the 1930s inspired by Rembrandt, El Greco and Dürer. The result is a remarkable if still unappreciated book. Its references to Renaissance artists and their styles of representation are too difficult for the ordinary reader to disentangle. The title story, set in the present day, is an amplification of her story about Rembrandt. The protagonist is Nathanaël, a young man who gains access to the household staff of the Van Herzog family on a remote Frisian island. He communes with several paintings on their walls, and then merges with, even vanishes into, the sea himself, a figure on a still-life canvas who is no longer able to differentiate between the reality of his own mundane life and the exquisite seascape scenes on the paintings he dusts.[91] Yourcenar also tidied up her anthology of 100 ancient poets, which Gallimard would soon bring out entitled *The Crown and the Lyre*.

Yukio Mishima (1925–70) was born in Tokyo, distinguished himself studying law, and published his first novel while still very young. He continued to write plays, novels and short stories, and in 1954 won the Shinchosha literary prize for his novel *The Sound of Waves*. He also travelled to America after World War Two, where he championed the traditions of Japan's imperial past in a fiercely anti-Japanese country because he believed this heritage was being eroded in the West. Mishima attempted a coup against the Japanese military with several members of his private Tate no Kai (Shield Society) army. When the attempt failed to drum up a following from within the ranks of infantrymen, the disillusioned Mishima took his own life. In 1970, aged just 45, he and a colleague committed hara-kiri (also called seppuku), ritual suicide by disembowelment. Many of his works deal with male sexual perfection in different guises, and with illicit love as the antidote to conventional values. *Forbidden Colours* is the story of Shunsuké's entanglement with the beautiful, graceful athlete Yuichi who is homosexual. Shunsuké realizes by turns that by bonding with Yuichi he can effect the terrible revenge on womankind he has been looking for, and thereby assuage the pain of his bitter marriages and broken heterosexual affairs. But Yuichi becomes an unwilling accomplice in the plot. Yourcenar's decision to write about Mishima came about as the convergence of enduring interests: her old habit of writing estimates of contemporary writers and charting the boundaries between their writing and behaviour, her lingering fascination with Oriental – especially Japanese – culture, and, not least, her attraction to Mishima's exotic blend of bravery, heroism and sensuality.

And between 1978 and 1981 she worked on a short but brilliantly incisive book about Yukio Mishima, a work as remarkable in every way as 'An Obscure Man'.

Yourcenar's *Vision of the Void* is a shrewd reappraisal of Mishima's life and times, only a step below her two masterpieces. She had read and marked up his novels in French translation for over two decades. His suicide in 1970 pierced her, as her correspondence reveals, causing her to peruse more of his works. Here she was as attracted to his exhibitionism, homosexuality, sadism, voyeurism, as when she comments: *In the first scene of his {Mishima's} first ejaculation before a photograph of Guido Reni's* St Sebastian, *the excitement derived from Italian Baroque painting is the more understandable insofar as Japanese art, even in its erotic engravings, never indulged, as did Western art, in the glorification of the nude. That muscular body {of Mishima} driven to exhaustion {masturbating} collapsed in the almost voluptuous abandon of agony, would not have appeared in any depiction of a samurai put to death.*[92]

Mishima, Zeno, Hadrian: she had imagined herself as all three, especially in their erotics and their manner of death. She construed Mishima's sexual ecstasy as kindred to that of Sade and Cocteau yet viewed him, above all, as a visionary voice preoccupied with the liberation of sensuality – of the kind she had just written about in 'An Obscure Man' – and with suicide and death, primary themes for her own oeuvre. Under altered circumstances Yourcenar herself could have been an early suicide, spectacularly staging her own death as did Mishima. Her book remains one of the most lucid statements to date about this visionary of 20th-century Oriental literature. It also demonstrates that the primary role of death and reincarnation in her own oeuvre had not diminished after *The Abyss*. It intensified while she watched her conjugal partner dying on Mount Desert.

The book about Mishima also heightened her consuming interest in the Orient, especially in Japan. She began to ponder what else she might write about Mishima and extended her explorations by translating five of his Noh plays, which appeared in 1984. All this while Grace gasped for breath from her deathbed. By January 1979 Frick was entirely immobile; by October fading. She died on 18 November and was cremated on the island.

There is a passage in Jensen's *Gradiva* (1903), published in the year of both Grace's and Yourcenar's birth and which Marguerite had read, describing Gradiva's rebirth. Freud was deeply inspired by Jensen's account for the way it explained a universal psychic renewal. The story could as well have been applied to Marguerite: while Grace lived Marguerite was protective, would let no one else translate her into English. She could be appallingly inflexible to her partner yet remained loyal. But once Grace was gone all changed and the belle of Mont Noir was ready to tap-dance again, this time not with another woman but with young Jerry Wilson. And so she did, as the daybooks reveal. She rearranged the house, discarded furniture, locked up Grace's piano, threw away Grace's clothing and possessions. Most noteworthy was her frenzy to hit the road. She had been unable to travel for a decade because of Grace's illness. But, now there was Jerry, a world-class traveller himself and easy match for her nomadism.

Within weeks of Grace's death in November 1979 a debate was heating up in Paris about her earlier nomination, which Yourcenar heard about only second-hand. Camps for and against her election had formed and were solidifying: a tragi-comedy that would play itself out for almost a year. Every possible objection was raised by the opposition, including the charge that she was ineligible because she was Belgian and the equally absurd claim that she was now American because she had become a naturalized citizen in 1947 (and received an American passport in 1948). Yourcenar, though she had been born in Brussels and had gone to live in America, was still clearly French in her head and heart – not least by virtue of her writing exclusively in that language. The pro-Yourcenar faction, equally strong, championed her on grounds that she produced literature of the highest quality, standards for which the Académie itself had been founded in 1634. It did not hurt that an English woman (Margaret Thatcher) on the other side of the English Channel had been named Prime Minister a few months earlier; if Britain could have a female leader at its helm, France's Académie Française could elevate one woman into its ranks. Marguerite herself adopted a posture of indifference, claiming she had not sought the elevation and was bored by the whole affair, which further endeared her to her constituency. When the time came to vote, Yourcenar prevailed.

She could have had no better pretext for new travels. She was summoned to install herself in Paris at once: for interviews, press releases, and, of course, the final ceremony on 22 January 1981 under the ancient dome at the Quai de Conti on the Left Bank.

> The Académie Française is the oldest institution rewarding intellectual and artistic distinction in France. Founded in 1634 it has been limited to 40 'Immortals' at any one time. Corneille and Racine were among its members. Ever since the 18th century women could be proposed, and several were, but they never received sufficient votes for election, which required a majority of the existing members. Yourcenar was the first woman to receive the necessary votes but it was a close count. She accumulated 20 votes out of 36 members who voted on that occasion. Her detractors, who vigorously campaigned against her before she succeeded, used smear techniques extending to her gender. One of the jokes they told after her election was that the Académie had gone to great expense to install a new female toilet.

A year before this she and Jerry had travelled in the American South, in part out of deference to Grace, with whom she had been there in the first few years after their arrival in America. Now Marguerite and Jerry went further afield, to England, France, Amsterdam and Bruges in 1981 and to Venice, Morocco, Egypt, Kenya, India and Japan in 1982. No place was too remote for the now decorated octogenarian and fair-haired southern boy much less than half her age. They visited James Baldwin, the African-American writer, in Saint Paul-de-Vence, the first of several visits. Jerry was eager to meet this famous gay writer; Marguerite got on so well with him that she translated his play *The Amen Corner* into French.

It remained to make a success of her new life with this young man. To all who could watch them it was clear that Jerry was no factotum but someone as integral to her and as necessary as Grace had been. Nevertheless, the relation was taxing. Yourcenar was tired. Jerry was devoted to her but spent his nights cruising in gay bars wherever they went. She grew possessive and jealous. They fought. A catalogue raisonné plotting their geographical movements and emotional (and sexual) entanglements would be an archive well worth having.

James Baldwin

Yourcenar continued to churn out books, but she was slowing down. Travel was tiring her. In 1983 Gallimard published *That Mighty Sculptor, Time*. Favourably reviewed in the London *Times Literary Supplement*, it was merely a collection of already published essays.[93] Next year, 1984, saw her joint publication with Jerry about gospel blues. Inspired by the trip they had taken to the American South, where Jerry could photograph the cotton fields, they conjured a book called *Blues and Gospels*. She wrote, or compiled, the text; he illustrated it. It was to be a coffee-table book, produced on expensive paper. Yourcenar gathered Negro spirituals: poems she had come to love from her darkest years after migrating to America. The surprise came in her autobiographical introduction. Here she recounted how she had met many African-Americans in the new world, especially in Harlem and in the South during the years she and Grace had lived in Manhattan and Hartford. Two decades earlier, in 1964, she had published a book about them called *Deep River, Dark River*, named after the Negro spiritual.

She claims that Negro spirituals work by casting magical spells; they were a type of the magic that interested her throughout her writing career. She went as far as proclaiming that African-Americans who composed the spirituals had influenced her in creating the figure of the Divine Father in *The Abyss*.[94] Gallimard published the book, tagged to a high price. Jerry had long since been installed at Petite Plaisance. Indeed, he moved in shortly after Grace's death. But fate again intervened: the same Ananke, or Greek Fate, Yourcenar had so adeptly deconstructed when retrieving the genealogy of the Crayencour dynasty in *The Labyrinth of the World*. Jerry was diagnosed with AIDS.

The clouds gathered again, as they had in 1939 when she was broke. From late 1984 to early 1986 Jerry deteriorated. His was a rather early diagnosis in the so-called gay plague then sweeping America. His boyfriend came to stay with him. Then they went together to New York to seek treatment. When that failed they moved to Paris, hoping an experimental clinic could help him and, again, leaving Yourcenar alone. But no remedy helped. Yourcenar characterized the time of the illness this way to her future biographer Josyanne Savigneau: *the entire year 1985 – along with two months that preceded it and followed it – was a long, dark tale of horror with very few bright spots.*[95] Dark it was. She barely managed to read the proofs of the English translation of her *Oriental Tales*, appearing in America for the first time.

Jerry would prove to be irreplaceable. For five decades

Yourcenar had lived a highly regimented routine, spending long hours alone in her office reading and writing. When she surfaced she wanted company: people with good conversation who would nevertheless let her hold court. Their discourse had to be informed and critical, as was hers, but they must also recognize that she – not they – was the wordsmith and that writing, as novelist Laurence Sterne had quipped in *Tristram Shandy*, was but a type of conversation managed well. Talk, good talk, was the very stuff of her free hours, the day's pudding. Grace had not merely been a consummate listener in the good years; she knew how to make Marguerite soar in the telling of stories and knew how important it was to keep quiet when guests visited. Like Grace, Jerry also possessed this amazing talent for talk. And he also spoke French. He was becoming the joy of her life: handsome, cultured, sensitive, male, and young. Once he was gone she would be terminally alone. At 83 she was too old to replace her companion yet again.

By the time Jerry died on 8 February 1986 at the Laennec Clinic in Paris her own words were no longer flowing as quickly as they had. A few small strokes had impaired her. Writers throughout history have done well into their 70s; after 80, their fields of vision become much narrower. She noticed she was forgetting things, even the meaning of ordinary words in French. The last thing she dreamed was that she would outlive both Grace and Jerry. Something in her died when Jerry did, but she mustered the energy to return to Europe. The pretext was that she wanted to see some old friends again and, especially, visit Jorge Luis Borges, about whose works Professor Walter Kaiser had persuaded her to give a lecture at Harvard the following October (1987). She found Borges weary, ready to die (he died a few weeks later on 14 June), and was immensely moved by the meeting.

The rest of 1986 was as chaotic but not entirely solitary: at least for one as reliant on conversation as she was. Having returned that

June to Petite Plaisance, she decided she could no longer stay there. In Paris she had met an elderly African nurse called Monicah who agreed to accompany her on further European travels. Marguerite paid for everything. She tried to carry on working but nothing came: neither ideas nor words. Was it the loss of conversation? Still, she soldiered on. The pressing plan that summer was to return to Europe with someone, for the idea of her travelling alone was impossible. Having identified and cajoled candidates, she settled on Monicah, returned to Paris, and saw many of the old crowd, especially those who had campaigned for her election to the Académie. But she was tired and sick. Her friends often had to take her back to the hotel early and put her to bed.

She remained in Paris all winter. She was now 83. The memory of Grace was fading and flickering; even Jerry seemed a thing of the past. She rallied in the summer of 1987: perhaps, she thought, she could make a life for herself after all, relocate to Paris, find some new project. Now, in her last year, she even conjured a

Yourcenar photographed by Sophie Bassonis at Petite Plaisance, Maine

fourth volume in the *The Labyrinth of the World* series. Her October lecture at Harvard went off well enough, but she returned to Maine tired and with a pain in the back. Complications set in and by November she was in the Bar Harbor Hospital. The diagnosis was uncertain, perhaps even as minor as the old hypochondria. Whatever her medical case history, which has never been charted, and whether she had been struck by cardiac arrest or stroke or some combination of the two, she lost the life force. She had little left for which to live. Under these circumstances corporeal matter even as seemingly durable and indestructible as hers gives up.

Her Paris friends grew alarmed. Several threatened to take the first plane across the Atlantic. A few actually arrived. But it was too late. By early December she was too confused to talk to anyone. She died peacefully, tranquillized in room 114 on the evening of 17 December in her 84th year, her ambitions mostly fulfilled. By now she was firmly written into history as she had always wanted to be. Her life had been validated despite all the odds. She had spent over four decades on a remote island but France – all of France – had finally awakened to her achievement and elevated her to a place she thought she well deserved. No honour seemed too great. Had she been nominated for a Nobel Prize she would have accepted. She did not seek out honours but when they arrived she basked. If only papa Michel, and perhaps Grace too, could see her now.

Her reception in the decade after her death (1987–97) would make for another book, perhaps called *The Unmaking of Marguerite Yourcenar*, contrasting the undying adulation of her followers with the critiques of many academic feminists and gay critics. Nevertheless Yourcenar succeeded in preserving her individuality and ensuring that she would become part of history. Despite advice to shape herself this way or that, in life and literature, she steadfastly refused and remained her idiosyncratic self to the very end. Like Hadrian, she wanted to be remembered for her works, not evaporate from memory, so took great care to preserve every scrap, every note, every letter sent to or from her. She wrote her best work late in life, after allowing it to mellow for many years, even decades. Her first important book appeared when she was almost 50. The ebb of time between conception and execution of a book gave a maturity to her vision that not all great writers enjoy. She wrote about lands vanished from contemporary maps, forgotten people from past times. Yet the lights of Greece and Rome cast long shadows on her plots, and her portraits of Hadrian and Zeno, and perhaps Alexis and Nathanaël also, remain the most compelling appearances in literature of figures of these types. It is hard to think of another writer of the 20th century who could have captured Hadrian as well as she did. She entered history impassively, brilliantly re-creating its figures while remaining apart from them. Like a painter of still life, she captured the essences of her subjects in a single stroke or with one dash of paint. Yet she herself – the consummate painter of character, the flesh-and-blood writer – always kept herself far removed from the canvas's centre. Peter Kemp has summarized her heroes well: 'Like all Yourcenar's characters they are at once intensely individual and still held in the matrix of history.'[96] She too is now held in that universal matrix.

Epilogue: Is Yourcenar a Gay Writer?

Marguerite Yourcenar was born into an ancient Catholic family, but neither her father Michel nor she ever practised conventional Christianity. From the time they moved to Paris after World War One Marguerite almost never entered a Christian church, except to admire its architecture, nor did she believe in the tenets of Christianity. If she had any religion – a big if – it was a personal one: an eclectic blend of pagan, mystic, ancient Greek and Zen Buddhist beliefs. Like Hadrian and Zeno, into whose characters she poured so much of herself, she was never a traditional Christian. She neither condoned Christianity's views of 'normal' sexuality nor would have endorsed its condemnation of homosexuality.

The biographical facts of her sexuality are sometimes overlooked. Classified in any clinical or – worse yet – pathological sense, Marguerite Yourcenar was bisexual. During her life she actively seduced both women and men and fell madly in love with both. She was not interested in a science of sex, nor thought it able to solve the mystery of sexual attraction; and she apparently read nothing about biology or genetics. The biographical fact that she hitched her stars to a woman – Grace Frick – may have been as accidental as it was fortuitous for her career, for it is unlikely that many others, of either gender, would have cared for her as much as Grace did. Yourcenar could be equally indifferent to disparities of age. Her early male lovers during the 1930s in Europe were generally about her own age. But American Jerry Wilson was much less than half it. Yet there can be no doubt that her attraction to him was, in part, sexual, and may even have been consummated. We may never know.

Yet Yourcenar made a claim about women in literature that cost her a great deal among feminist and gay readers. She wrote: *it was virtually impossible to take a feminine character as a central figure . . . Women's lives are much too limited, or else too secret.*[97] The comment has been construed by a wide variety of recent critics[98] as failure and cowardice. Their argument proceeds as follows: Yourcenar believed that women could not be proper subjects for great themes; yet she was burning to celebrate homosexual love. She therefore transformed her women into men and, instead, celebrated male sexual love. But she was even too cowardly to accomplish this male celebration openly. For she distanced herself in time (ancient rather than modern) and place (Greece and Rome rather than France or America) and then entirely removed herself from her narratives. Her works are therefore deceptions on several levels: sexuality, gender and autobiography. They betray the cause of lesbian liberation, whose progress during her lifetime was remarkable. Yourcenar cannot be classified as a gay writer, as are Sylvia Townsend Warner (ten years Yourcenar's elder), Radclyffe Hall and Virginia Woolf for example, nor should she be. Yourcenar was no emancipator and must be relegated, in Gay Wachman's phrase, to the company of such 'lesbian cross-dressed narrators' as Mary Renault (1905–1983) and Winifred Bryher (1894–1983) who also 'cross-wrote' conservative historical novels which distanced their authors from their narratives.[99] What is more, Yourcenar also distanced herself from the high Modernism of her epoch, which Woolf and company did not, and retreated instead into a nostalgic form of Romantic literature couched in classical prose. Her works belong to the era of Gide and Mann, the claim goes, rather than Warner and Woolf.

Did Yourcenar hide her true self? Survey her work and you find that her secretiveness rarely extends to the kingdom of sex. Her personal credo, like Hadrian's – or the Hadrian she wanted to believe in – celebrates carnal sex. She had no reason to hide the temptations of the flesh, which she considered ecstatic and liberating rather than repressive. Nothing in her oeuvre is more joyous than the mutual sexual love of Hadrian and Antinous.

She was, nevertheless, a figure who lived at a specific historical moment. She practised bisexuality openly and, if interrogated off the record, did not conceal the fact. But she was raised in an aesthetic milieu in which art and life were strictly separated and she continued to believe in their separation. She believed to her last day that a writer's personal sexuality had nothing to do with her art or level of accomplishment. She was no puritan. But she drew a fixed border between her life and her art and rarely permitted others to trespass across it.

Yourcenar matured at a time when lesbian women were coming into their own. She knew this lesbian world, especially in Europe, and some of its inhabitants knew her. The salons of such women as Natalie Barney and Colette were well aware that Yourcenar was a lesbian woman who sexually recruited other women. But whereas most others in these lesbian salons celebrated the loves of women in their books, Yourcenar did not. The reasons are more complex, and sometimes more biographical, than labels such as 'lesbian cross-dresser' or 'transvestite narrator' suggest. They include her early identification with her father and his desperate need for a son who could succeed in the way Marguerite did; her unquenchable thirst for glory and attendant, unwarranted, sense that women had been noteworthy, but not great, in history; her dislike of domesticity and quaint sentiment, which she equated with women, as distinct from noble and sublime emotion which she deemed to be masculine; and the fact that she could be sexually active among men, almost promiscuously so, as she was in the beginning of her life and may have been at the end with Jerry Wilson. A psychoanalyst might say she introjected her composite disdain for women, turning her disdain for women against herself and assuming the persona of a male.

Yourcenar became a celebrity in America during the peak of the Gay Liberation movement of the 1960s and 1970s. Despite her seclusion on an island, the gay movement – on both sides of the Atlantic – was well aware that this cultural icon was living with another woman. They implored her to disclose the truth. She flatly refused, as adamantly as she refrained from celebrating the loves of female equivalents of Hadrian and Zeno. (When Matthieu Galey interviewed her on the island for days and days to produce *With Open Eyes*, she told him all sorts of things about her sexuality, never thinking he would put them into the book. He did so and the result filled her with disgust and horror.) Instead she developed a theory about the Greek poet Sappho: in her correspondence, in the poems by Sappho she translated, and in a more than usually candid chapter about female homosexuality in her book of interviews called *With Open Eyes*.[100] This was the view that lesbian women of the past, especially Sappho, had been largely silent. Hence it was too difficult, if not altogether impossible, to retrieve their voices. In this she was wrong, whether or not the women were homosexual. Fictional and real women such as Phèdre, Medea, Lady Macbeth, Mary Queen of Scots, even Sappho, whatever the nature of their sexuality, and many others far less known, can be and are being retrieved. Nor were all mute about their sexuality. The discoveries of the last generation have controverted Yourcenar's position: lesbian history is now a flourishing subject producing many articles and books each year that discover new figures whose voices were not silent.

The lesbian movement, in Europe and America, passed Yourcenar by. The ceremony elevating her as an 'Immortal' of the Académie Française occurred within weeks of the detection of the first case of AIDS in the winter of 1981. After Yourcenar returned to Mount Desert that year her preoccupation lay in making some type of life with young Jerry Wilson. 'Coming out' as a lesbian, even an octogenarian lesbian, was the furthest intention from her mind. The pressures of AIDS lifted the lid off female as well as male sexuality. The resulting openness ended the silence of women in history, which Yourcenar theorized about. Never again would women be so mute.

It was too late for Yourcenar. She who never answered to anyone in the professional workplace, and whose pride was second only to secretiveness in her emotional chemistry, was barely qualified to lead marches for lesbian toleration and same sex compassion. Ironically after her elevation as an Immortal she was routinely asked what she thought, and was pleased to give her opinions. When her opinions, especially her post-election views, are collected and assessed, it becomes clear that she stood, on the one hand, for women's rights (the right to abortion, care for single mothers and equality for women in the workplace), and, on the other, for the continued privacy of the individual, including her own. She never changed her views about female silence, especially sexual silence.

The conventional wisdom today is that gay writers are those who publicly celebrate same-sex intimacy and love from friendship and discipleship to romantic intimacy and erotic attachment: the same-sex equivalents of the variety of heterosexual unions. Feminist critics have laid bare the issue. Their requirement is open allegiance to the cause – hence their 'Sapphistries' (the phrase is Susan Gubar's) – without disguise, distance or deception. By this yardstick Yourcenar fails the D-word test: she practised all three in her writing.

In 1979 Georges Stambolian, an academic scholar in America, interviewed leading American theatre critic Eric Bentley about the state of homosexuality in literature.[101] This was just as the debate about Yourcenar's election to the Académie Française was heating up in Paris and virtually at the peak of her international celebrity. Bentley, speaking frankly, even autobiographically, commented this way about Yourcenar, especially the narrator in the *Memoirs of*

Hadrian: 'it is a woman speaking, and speaking about a great man and his lover.' Yourcenar, if she could have overheard the interview, would have vigorously objected to the notion that she was a female voyeur glamorizing male erotic love. Instead – she would have interjected – history revealed the great male love of these two figures, old and young. She was always ready to admit that she had not been present. Was this a reply?

Bentley continued by comparing her to Mary Renault. 'They are both on a power trip. Madly identifying themselves with male power. If it is remarkable, in this day and age, to make much of Antinous and Bagoas [Renault's homosexual boy in *The Persian Boy* (1956)], it is even more remarkable that a woman should make much of Alexander or Hadrian.' Yourcenar would have lashed out furiously at the folly of attributing these motives to her. The idea that she was identifying with these great men of the past to enhance her own cult status and glory was one thing; to accuse her of 'madly' collapsing her own identity into that of these great men another.

The point epitomizes the debate that has continued since 1979 and heated up since Yourcenar's death about the relation of her oeuvre to gay literature of the 20th century. Since then gay literature has established itself as a major form of modern writing, not merely in colleges and universities, but among readers and writers throughout the world. This small volume has said rather little about Yourcenar as a 'gay writer'. She herself would have loathed the categorization, as firmly as she opposed the classification of human beings according to the gender of their sexual object choice. She was much too ruggedly individualistic, or eccentric, to divide people into sexual stereotypes. Whereas she championed the Negro cause in America in the 1950s (at a time when you could still use that word) because theirs was a crusade for the freedom of the human soul, she was much less enthusiastic about liberating same-sex desire, the fulfilment of which, she thought, remained within the control of each person's free will. Human beings, she believed, carve their own destinies, as she had sculpted hers. Should they desire *sensuality* – her consistent term for sexual union – with members of their own sex, they could achieve it by deciding to engage in it. It was as simple as that. The decision to do so, she further believed, could hardly constitute the basis for the distinction in writing one had, or had not, achieved. Greatness in that realm was the product of talent, application, erudition, industry, unrelenting revision, and, most of all, the almost Nietzschean will to be a writer.

Still, the post-1987 world since her death has enthroned gay writing. All over the world bookshops have dedicated wings; readers have developed an innate sense of what a 'gay writer' is. It is fair game to ask whether or not Yourcenar was one. She would have recoiled, I think, to read this epilogue and the questions it raises. The love between two persons, she believed, was gender-free, immortal, timeless, and certainly magical and mystical. It had neither name nor gender. Besides, she had aspired to be a great writer, not a great lover. So why was this question being put in the first place? Her goal was the attainment of classic status, and she had defined what that entailed at the start of her essay about Thomas Mann: *The works of Thomas Mann have attained to that very rare category, the modern classic; that is to say, they are among productions still recent and still open to debate, but worthy of being taken up again and again for examination and reconsideration in all their aspects and at every level of their meaning; they serve to nourish the mind, but to test it, as well.*[102]

She had opinions about everything. She would have chastised us not to inquire whether Mann or Gide were gay writers. She was too proud to seek a temporary niche among academic critics seeking to recruit her for a category (lesbian historian) or ideological cause (feminism), or who were worried that they would find her neutral in her versions of modernism or insufficiently 'gay' because she did not celebrate the loves of women in her books. In this sense she remained, in Terry Castle's phrase,[103] an apparitional lesbian: no gay writer at all.

The crucial issue about Yourcenar, however, is not whether she was apparitional or an overtly gay writer but what type of writer she was in the first place. The concerns of French commentator François Sureau include some of the issues about which sides must be taken, pro or con: 'That attitude she has – the great writer polishing her status (just look at her biography in the Pléiade) – with her solitude on one side, her opinions about everything on the other, the high-flown airs she puts on . . . perhaps all this makes me unfair. Her style is cold, heavy, and provincial, her philosophy is ponderous, but there are some fine things ...'.[104] Sureau has a point, harsh though it is. Many feminists have agreed with him since he wrote not so very long ago in 1989.

Many of these women, however, overlook the numbers of male writers since Thomas Mann who have found great virtues in Yourcenar's writing. A proper list would include many authors beyond the realm of the expected: Mishima (who thought *Memoirs of Hadrian* one of the great French novels of his time), William Styron (who found Yourcenar technically flawless, a model to be followed), and Lawrence Durrell (who praised Yourcenar in many lectures throughout Europe). What has not yet occurred is the conversion of the feminists. Female adherents of Yourcenar are few and far between, and when they exist they do not lucidly give their reasons. If the criterion is women of national or international literary stature, then the numbers of devotees are fewer yet. Change the condition once more to lesbian feminists and the cry of battle commences for all the reasons I have enumerated in this chapter. Ultimately it may be that Yourcenar's enduring reputation will be made or broken by those of her own sex.

I could not have predicted this state of affairs in 1961, or even 1981. The idea that imaginative literature should be judged entirely according to its ideological value was alien to me. Now, over two decades after 1981, I keep wondering if Yourcenar's contemporary 'sisters', as it were, will provide reasons for her niche or defend a label (i.e., gay writer, straight writer) to describe her achievement and enduring worth. I have offered a personal account but my biographically based exploration does not extend far enough. The question about her status as a gay writer does not penetrate to the heart of Yourcenar country. For this one must look elsewhere, to her representations of secrecy and magic: the key to her view of the human condition.

All Yourcenar's writing, like the pillars of her life, thrives on magic and disguise: this is why her male heroes are obsessed with the occult and secrecy. Yourcenar's literary greatness is not primarily based on the celebration of homosexual love but on her penetration of the human condition through intuitive avenues of mystery and magic. In this she was a thoroughly original voice. Hadrian succeeds in both the public and the private realms, as emperor and lover, by his staunch refusal to surrender to the forces of reason. Zeno's life is steeped in occultism; it, in turn, saves him from detection by the Inquisition and permits him to understand why suicide is the best of his options. Yourcenar's own memoirs and correspondence with others reveal the woman she fundamentally was: inquisitive and intuitive, forever secretive, obsessed with the past, persuaded that the human being is great by virtue of mystical and occult qualities that do not die when the physical body decomposes. In this sense she was as much a latter-day Neo-Platonist as a 'gay writer'. Only her protagonist Alexis privileges sexual orientation as the monumental challenge of his life. However well-crafted a book *Alexis* is, it is not Yourcenar's most distinctive work. If it had been, or if it had been her only fiction, her literary reputation would be a fraction of what it justly should be.

Yet even this conclusion to my personal approach to her life and works does not extend far enough, for Yourcenar's biography is so inextricably implicated in her writing that the two cannot be separated. Life, for her, was writing, and vice-versa. In eighty-four years, which had been blessed by a superior genetic pool that permitted good health, as well as economic means and retreat to America to practice her craft, she craved three fundamental states: 1. the freedom to love members of both sexes; 2. the liberty to explore the irrational sides of the human condition in ways ranging from the mystical to the occult and spiritual, usually in historical settings; 3. the ability to keep travelling – to be on the road as a way of life. Same-sex romantic love figures of course, but you could still have the essential Yourcenar if her heroes were not bisexual or homosexual.

Yourcenar herself – if she could return from the dead – would continue to maintain she was *not* a gay novelist. Her sin was that she wanted to *be* Hadrian – to *be* a great man – and pretended to do so. But *being* Hadrian was not equivalent to being gay: neither in her view nor the critics'. She insisted many times, in language that makes the point even if it did not use these words. Even in denial, she practised secretiveness and could not bring herself to use vulgarisms like gay. Her position must not, of course, count for much. The fact that Yourcenar continues to disclaim her status as a gay writer is merely one strain among many. It derives as much from her practice of disguise and cult of secrecy as other sources. More consequential is that she was a bisexual woman who wrote a sizable body of literature, much of which darkly confronts the human condition, little of which can be properly called gay.

Notes

1. Barnes, Julian, *Flaubert's Parrot* (London: 1984), p 2.
2. Savigneau, Josyanne, *Marguerite Yourcenar: Inventing a Life*, tr Joan E Howard (New York: 1991).
3. 'Reflections on the Composition of the *Memoirs of Hadrian*' in Yourcenar, Marguerite, *Memoirs of Hadrian*, tr Grace Frick (New York: 1963).
4. Wachman, Gay, *Lesbian Empire* (New Brunswick: 2001), p 190.
5. There is currently a debate about the authorship of this painting among Rembrandt specialists but Yourcenar had no doubt that it was his.
6. See Saint, Nigel, *Marguerite Yourcenar: Reading the Visual* (Oxford: 2000).
7. Savigneau, *Yourcenar*, p 527.
8. Savigneau, *Yourcenar*, p 428.
9. Quoted in Savigneau, *Yourcenar*, p 87.
10. Savigneau, *Yourcenar*, p 167.
11. As documented in her Pléiade Chronology (1982).
12. Savigneau, *Yourcenar*, pp x–xii.
13. Yourcenar, *With Open Eyes*, tr Arthur Goldhammer (Boston: 1984) p 19.
14. Yourcenar, *Dear Departed*, tr Maria Louise Ascher (New York: 1991) pp 145–242.
15. Barnes, *Flaubert's Parrot*, p 187.
16. Yourcenar, *With Open Eyes*, chapter 1.
17. The most reliable source for her first ten years of life is her autobiographical *Dear Departed* (New York: 1991).
18. Yourcenar, *With Open Eyes*, p 10.
19. Yourcenar, *With Open Eyes*, p 16.
20. Yourcenar, *With Open Eyes*, p 30.
21. Yourcenar, *With Open Eyes*, p 31.
22. Yourcenar, *Memoirs of Hadrian*, p 274.
23. Yourcenar, *With Open Eyes*, p 35.
24. Yourcenar, *With Open Eyes*, pp 33–35.
25. Harvard Collection, unpublished letter to Denys Magne, 15 April 1973.

26 Yourcenar, 'Reflections on the Composition of the *Memoirs of Hadrian*' in *Memoirs of Hadrian*, p 126.
27 Yourcenar, *How Many Years*, tr Maria Louise Ascher (New York: 1995) p 284.
28 In *Bibliothèque Universelle et Revue de Genève*, no 68 (June), pp 745–52.
29 Yourcenar, *Alexis*, tr Walter Kaiser (New York: 1984) p 75.
30 See the chapter on *Alexis* in *With Open Eyes*, pp 43–49.
31 Savigneau, *Yourcenar*, p 79.
32 *Revue Bleue*, no 20 (19 October), pp 621–27.
33 *Les Nouvelles Littéraires*, 29 April 1930.
34 Jorge Carlos Borges, *Collected Essays* (1954), quoted in Savigneau, *Yourcenar*, p 428.
35 Yourcenar, *With Open Eyes*, p 58.
36 Yourcenar, *Pindar*, p 284, translation mine.
37 Yourcenar, *With Open Eyes*, p 60.
38 An interview between Fraigneau and Savigneau, quoted in Savigneau, *Yourcenar*, p 92.
39 In *Fires*, in her play *To Each his Minotaur*, and in her memoir *The Labyrinth of the World*.
40 All the below passages are found in Savigneau, *Yourcenar*, pp 102–3.
41 Isherwood, Christopher, *Goodbye to Berlin* (London: 1939), p 51.
42 Savigneau, *Yourcenar*, p 137.
43 Yourcenar, *Memoirs of Hadrian*, p 274.
44 See Yourcenar, *Memoirs of Hadrian*, p 275; Yourcenar, *With Open Eyes*, p 118.
45 Yourcenar, *Memoirs of Hadrian*, p 139. For the comment about meeting Hadrian see Savigneau, *Yourcenar*, p 324.
46 Savigneau, *Yourcenar*, p 222, notes that Plon issued almost 100,000 copies of it by 1958; by 1989 the number had swelled to almost one million.
47 Yourcenar, *Memoirs of Hadrian*, p 119.
48 Yourcenar, *Memoirs of Hadrian*, p 211.
49 Yourcenar, *Memoirs of Hadrian*, p 233.
50 See Savigneau, *Yourcenar*, p 265.
51 Yourcenar, *Memoirs of Hadrian*, p 269.
52 Auden, W H, *Age of Anxiety: a baroque eclogue* (New York: 1947).
53 Yourcenar, *Memoirs of Hadrian*, p 78.
54 Yourcenar, *Memoirs of Hadrian*, p 271.
55 Yourcenar, *With Open Eyes*, p 117.
56 Savigneau, *Yourcenar*, pp 176–77.

57 Savigneau, *Yourcenar*, p 177.
58 See Yourcenar, *With Open Eyes*, pp 125–26.
59 Yourcenar, *Memoirs of Hadrian*, p 159.
60 Yourcenar, *Memoirs of Hadrian*, p 274.
61 Yourcenar, *Memoirs of Hadrian*, p 274.
62 Syme, Ronald, *Fictional History Old and New: Hadrian – The James Bryce Memorial Lecture for 1984 at Somerville College* (Oxford: 1986) p 8.
63 Yourcenar, *Memoirs of Hadrian*, p 127.
64 Yourcenar, *Memoirs of Hadrian*, p 24.
65 Yourcenar, *Memoirs of Hadrian*, p 247.
66 Quoted in Heilbut, Anthony, *Thomas Mann: Eros and Literature* (New York: 1995) p 467.
67 Jens, I (ed), *Thomas Manns Tagebücher: 1953–55* (Frankfurt: 1995), p 537.
68 Mann, Erika, *Thomas Manns Briefe 1948–55 und Nachlese* (Frankfurt: 1965) p 316.
69 Jens, *Thomas Manns Tagebücher: 1953–55* (Frankfurt: 1995), p 537.
70 Their correspondence is in the Harvard Collection; see Sarde, Michèle, et al, *Marguerite Yourcenar: Lettres à ses amis et quelques autres* (Paris: 1995) pp 143–44.
71 Heilbut, *Thomas Mann*, p 467.
72 'Humanism and Occultism in Thomas Mann', tr Grace Frick, in *The Dark Brain of Piranesi and Other Essays* (New York: 1984), p 217.
73 Jens, *Thomas Manns Tagebücher: 1953–55* (Frankfurt: 1995), p 313.
74 Yourcenar, *The Abyss*, tr Grace Frick (New York: 1976), p 11.
75 Yourcenar, *The Abyss*, p 248.
76 See the 'Author's Note', Yourcenar, *The Abyss*, p 374.
77 See the 'Author's Note', Yourcenar, *The Abyss*, pp 362–67.
78 Yourcenar, *The Abyss*, p 183.
79 Yourcenar, *The Abyss*, p 475.
80 Kerényi, C, *Eleusis: Archetypal Image of Mother and Daughter* (London: 1967) p 67.
81 Kerényi, *Eleusis*, pp 101–36.
82 Kerényi, *Eleusis*, p 211.
83 Kerényi, *Eleusis*, pp 40–65.
84 See Eliade, Mircea, *Forgerons et alchimistes* (Paris: 1956) p 130.
85 See Savigneau, *Yourcenar*, pp 304–7.
86 See Sarde et al, *Marguerite Yourcenar: Lettres*, pp 372–494.
87 Unpublished letter to Michel Aubrion, 19 March 1970.

88 Letter dated 7 July 1939, quoted in Jonathan Fryer, *Christopher Isherwood* (New York: 1977), p 191.
89 See Savigneau, *Yourcenar*, p 770.
90 Yourcenar, *With Open Eyes*, p 174.
91 Saint, Nigel, *Marguerite Yourcenar: Reading the Visual* (Oxford: 2000) provides a splendid study of this novel.
92 Yourcenar, *Mishima: A Vision of the Void*, tr by Alberto Manguel (New York: 1986) p 7.
93 *Times Literary Supplement* (3 March 1984) p 156.
94 Yourcenar, *The Abyss*, p 3.
95 Quoted in Savigneau, *Yourcenar*, p 422.
96 Peter Kemp, 'Intensely Individual', *Times Literary Supplement* (21 February 1986), p 194.
97 Yourcenar, *Memoirs of Hadrian*, p 327.
98 Wachman, Gay, *Lesbian Empire: radical crosswriting in the Twenties* (New Brunswick: 2001), pp 1, 7, 39, 190; Doan, Laura L, *Fashioning Sapphism: the Origins of a Modern English Lesbian Culture* (New York: 2001), pp 95–125; Castle, Terry, *The Apparitional Lesbian: Female Homosexuality and Modern Culture* (New York: 1993); Benstock, Shari, *Women on the Left Bank: 1900–1940* (London: 1986).
99 Wachman, Gay, *Lesbian Empire*, p 190.
100 See Sarde et al, *Marguerite Yourcenar: Lettres*, pp 141, 233–4, 701–03; Yourcenar, *La Couronne et la lyre* (Paris: 1979) pp 69–83; Yourcenar, *With Open Eyes*, p 143. See also her letter to Suzanne Lilar about Sappho dated 19 May 1963 included in Sarde et al, *Marguerite Yourcenar: Lettres*, pp 230–35.
101 Bentley, Eric, 'We are in History: An Interview' in G Stambolian, *Homosexualities and French Literature* (Ithaca NY: 1979), p 131.
102 Yourcenar, *The Dark Brain of Piranesi*, p 199.
103 Castle, Terry, *The Apparitional Lesbian* (New York:1993).
104 François Sureau, *Garçon de quoi écrire* [Waiter, Something to Write With] (Paris: 1989), p 89.

Chronology

Year	Age	Life
1903		8 June, Marguerite born at 193 Avenue Louise in Brussels, Belgium, to Michel de Crayencour and Fernande de Cartier de-Marchienne. Ten days later her mother dies. Given name Marguerite Antoinette Jeanne Marie Ghislaine de Crayencour. Registered as French citizen. July, arrives at Mont Noir, near Lille, France, her father's estate.
1904	1	Living with father and German servant at Mont Noir, taught by father, does not attend school.
1910	7	Still at Mont Noir, taught by father, not attending school.
1911	8	Begins to study Latin; read Racine's *Phèdre*.
1912	9	Father Michel sells Mont Noir, buys apartment in Paris on the Avenue d'Antin in the first arrondissement.
1914	11	Father and daughter flee Paris for England; resident for nearly a year in Richmond, near London; Yourcenar visits the British Museum, sees the bronze bust of the Emperor Hadrian.
1915	12	Returns to Paris; summers in Provence.
1917	14	First poetic compositions.
1919	16	Privately educated, she passes her baccalaureat examinations at age 16 in Nice.
1921	18	Assumes name 'Yourcenar', an anagram of Crayencour, and uses it in the publication of her first work, *The Garden of Illusions*.
1922	19	Publication of *The Gods are not Dead*.
1929	26	Death of her father Michel on 12 January; publication of *Alexis*; receives the Prix René Vivien established by Natalie Clifford Barney of the Acadèmie des Femmes in Paris at the end of the year
1930	27	Travels widely in Europe
1931	28	Publication of *The New Eurydice*; travels to Switzerland, Italy, Greece, and lives on Aegean Sea island
1932	29	Publication of *Pindar*
1933	30	Nomadic travels in southern Europe
1934	31	*Death Drives the Cart* and *A Coin In Nine Hands*
1935	32	In love with Lucy Kyriakos
1936	33	Publication of *Fires*.
1937	34	Still traveling widely in Europe; meets Grace Frick, who had been born on 12 January 1903
1938	35	*Oriental Tales* and *Dreams and Destinies*; translates Virginia Woolf's *The Waves*
1939	36	Publishes *Le Coup de Grace*; travels widely in Europe; in Paris by September looking for a ship to America; flees Paris when the Germans invade early in September; in Bordeaux with Grace trying to find passage in an Atlantic ocean-liner; they sail on 14–15 October.

Year	History	Culture
1903	Suffragette movement begins in France. Wright Brothers' first flight.	Mann, *Tonio Krüger*, Henry James, *The Ambassadors*, Shaw, *Man and Superman*.
1904	Entente Cordiale signed between France and Britain.	Gourmont, *Promenades littéraires* (1904–13).
1910	George V becomes King of Britain.	Rabindranath Tagore, *Gitanjali*.
1911	Agadir crisis; constitutional crisis in UK.	Colette, *La Vagabonde*.
1912	*Titanic* sinks; French protectorate established over Morocco.	France, *Les Dieux ont soif*. Claudel, *L'Annonce fait à Marie*.
1914	Outbreak of World War One, Jaurès assassinated; Panama Canal opens. Péguy killed at the Battle of the Marne.	Proust, *A la recherche du temps perdu*. Gide, *Les caves du Vatican*. Joyce, *Dubliners*. Husserl, *Ideas*. Matisse painting.
1915	Fierce fighting on French soil.	Remy de Gourmont dies in Paris.
1917	Balfour Declaration. Russian Revolution.	Apollinaire, *Les Mamelles de Tirésias*.
1919	Treaty of Versailles. Nazi party founded. Mussolini founds Fascist movement.	Gide, *La Symphonie pastorale*. Valéry, *La Cimetière marin*. Colette, *Chéri*.
1921	French occupation of the Ruhr.	Cocteau, *Les Mariés de la Tour Eiffel*. Valéry, L'Ame et la danse.
1922	Poincaré elected French premier.	Montherland, *Le Songe*.
1929	Wall St crash. First all-fascist parliament in Italy. European Federal Union proposed.	Cocteau, *Les Enfants terribles*. Woolf, *Orlando*. Modigliani and Beckmann painting.
1930	Nazis elected to the Reichstag.	Freud, *Civilization and its Discontents*.
1931	Republic established in Spain.	Saint-Exupéry, *Vol de nuit*. Seferis, *Strophe*.
1932	Nazis gain more seats in the Reichstag.	Gris and Dufy painting.
1933	Hitler comes to power.	Malraux, *La Condition humaine*.
1934	Anti-republican riots in France.	Montherlant, *Les Célibataires*.
1935	Italian invasion of Abyssinia.	Guilloux, *Sang noir*.
1936	Spanish Civil War. Rhineland occupied.	Anouilh, *Le Voyageur sans bagages*.
1937	Blum government falls in France. Formation of Rome-Berlin Axis.	Malraux, *L'Espoir*. Breton, *L'Amour fou*. Edith Wharton dies in America.
1938	Austria succeeds to Germany as part of the Anschluss, Munich Agreement.	Sartre, *La Nausée*. Kazantzakis, *I Odysseia*.
1939	Germany occupies Czechoslovakia. Outbreak of World War Two.	Gracq, *Au Chateau d'Argol*. Sarraute, *Tropismes*. Sartre, *Le Mur*. Stravinsky, *Poetics of Music*.

Year	Age	Life
1940	37	Arrives in USA on New Year's Day with Grace Frick; settles with Frick into her Manhattan apartment at 448 Riverside Drive; Frick moves to 549 Prospect Avenue, West Hartford, Connecticut, to teach at Hartford Junior College.
1941	38	Yourcenar also moves to West Hartford; commutes to teach modern literature and languages part-time at Sarah Lawrence College in Westchester County, New York; writes nothing.
1942	39	Begins to teach classes at Sarah Lawrence College in Westchester County; *The Little Mermaid*, adapted from Hans Christian Andersen's tale, staged at Wadsworth Athenaeum, Hartford; first holiday spent on Mount Desert Island, Maine.
1943	40	Publishes nothing; first full summer on Mount Desert Island.
1944	41	Publishes a few more translations of Cavafy's poems in *Fontaine* and a short essay on 'Mythology' in *Les Lettres Françaises*, edited by Roger Caillois in Buenos Aires.
1945	42	Publishes nothing.
1946	43	Still teaching at Sarah Lawrence College
1947	44	Translates into French Henry James's *What Maisie Knew*, to which André Maurois writes a preface; becomes an American citizen under her now legal name Marguerite Yourcenar.
1948	45	Teaching and working on *Memoirs of Hadrian*.
1949	46	Still teaching; summer in Northeast Harbor on Mount Desert Island, Maine.
1950	47	Takes leave of absence from Sarah Lawrence College; meets Natalie Barney in Paris; several more trips to Mount Desert Island; Frick purchases Petite Plaisance on Mount Desert on 29 September.
1951	48	Plon publishes *Memoirs of Hadrian*.
1952	49	Frick translating *Memoirs of Hadrian* into English and discussing it almost daily with Yourcenar. Awarded the Prix Femina Vacaresco.
1953	50	Frick busy translating *Memoirs of Hadrian*.
1954	51	Frick's English translation of *Memoirs of Hadrian* published in New York by Farrar, Straus, & Giroux; book awarded the Page One Award by the Newspaper Guild of New York; publication of play *Electra or the Fall of the Masks*; extensive European travels, tour of Germany, university lectures.
1955	52	Winter in Var, France; *Electra* rehearsed in Paris for production but is aborted.
1956	53	Publication of *The Alms of Alcippus and other poems*.
1957	54	English translation of *Le Coup de Grâce*.
1958	55	Grace's breast cancer first diagnosed;
1959	56	Reading widely for *The Abyss*.
1960	57	Still reading.
1961	58	Writes *Rendre à Caesar* [Render unto Caesar]; honorary doctorate, Smith College, Northampton, Massachusetts.

Year	History	Culture
1940	Germans enter Paris, government moves to Vichy, Pétain becomes premier.	Hemingway, *For Whom the Bell Tolls*. Sartre, *L'Imaginaire*. Lorca, *A Poet in New York*. Hindemith composes Brecht's *Mother Courage* performed.
1941	Japanese attack Pearl Harbor.	
1942	Allies land in North Africa, Battle of El Alamein.	Eliot, *Four Quartets*. Camus, *L'Etranger* and *The Myth of, Sisyphus*. Fromm, *Fear of Freedom*.
1943	Germans surrender at Stalingrad.	Sartre, *Being and Nothingness*.
1944	Allied invasion of Normandy, Liberation of Paris and Vichy. Civil war in Greece.	Anouilh, *Antigone*. Jorge Luis Borges, *Fictions*. Eisenstein, *Ivan the Terrible*.
1945	Yalta Agreement, Germany surrenders.	Sartre, *The Age of Reason*.
1946	Fourth Republic in France.	Cocteau, *La belle e la bete*.
1947	India becomes independent.	Camus, *La Peste*. Genet, *Les Bonnes*. Gide wins Nobel Prize.
1948	Berlin airlift. Gandhi assasinated.	Mailer, *The Naked and the Dead*.
1949	NATO signed. People's Republic of China created. Council of Europe.	Sartre, *The Death of Love*. Orwell, *Nineteen Eighty-Four*.
1950	Schuman Plan. Korean War starts.	Camus, *Les Justes*. Ionesco, *The Bald Prima Donna*.
1951	Coal and Steel agreements in Europe. Anzus pact in the Pacific.	Camus, *L'Homme révolté*. Salinger, *Catcher in the Rye*. Gide dies.
1952	McCarthy era begins in USA.	Beckett, *Waiting for Godot*. Faulkner, *Requiem for a Nun*.
1953	Stalin dies. Korean War ends.	William Burroughs, *Junkie*.
1954	Algerian rebellion against France.	Amis, *Lucky Jim*. Messiaen and Shostakovich composing.
1955	Self-government in Tunisia.	Duras, *Le Square*. Robbe-Grillet, *Le Voyeur*.
1956	Anglo-French intervention in Suez.	Genet, *Le Balcon*. Camus, *La Chute*.
1957	Devaluation of French franc.	Camus wins Nobel Prize. Durrell, *The Alexandria Quartet* appears.
1958	De Gaulle elected French President.	Duras, *Moderato Cantabile*.
1959	Castro overthows Batista regime in Cuba.	Sarraute, *Le Planétarium*.
1960	Introduction of French new franc.	Ionesco, *Rhinoceros*.
1961	Algerian revolt collapses. Gagarin orbits earth.	Genet, *Les Paravents*. Tel Quel founded. Robbe-Grillet *Last Year in Marienbad*.

Year	Age	Life
1962	59	*Sous bénéfice d'inventaire*, published in English as *The Dark Brain of Piranesi*, awarded the Prix Combat.
1963	60	*The Mystery Play of Alcestis* and *To Each his Minotaur*.
1964	61	*Deep River, Dark River*, translations of Negro spirituals.
1965	62	Yourcenar at work on *The Abyss*.
1966	63	Yourcenar writing drafts of *The Abyss*.
1967	64	Reading proofs of *The Abyss* in Mount Desert.
1968	65	Publication of *The Abyss* (Paris: Gallimard) which is awarded a second Prix Femina; honorary doctorate, Bowdoin College, Maine; travels to Europe in the autumn.
1969	66	*A Critical Assessment of Hortense Flexner* published; Yourcenar remains in Europe until spring.
1970	67	Elected to the Belgian Académie Royale.
1971	68	In Belgium to give her inaugural lecture to the Belgian Académie; elected to the French Légion d'Honneur; publishes two volumes gathering her six plays.
1972	69	Wins a Prix Littéraire de Monaco; honorary doctorate, Colby College.
1973	70	
1974	71	Grand Prix National des Lettres, French Ministry of Culture; publication of *Dear Departed*, the first volume of her trilogy of memoirs, *The Labyrinth of the World*.
1975	72	No travels for almost a decade; Frick ill again but still translating.
1976	73	Frick's translation of *The Abyss* into English published.
1977	74	*The Abyss* is awarded a Grand Prix de l'Académie Française; publication of the second volume of *The Labyrinth of the World*, called *Archives du Nord*; *Le Coup de Grâce* made into a film by German director Volker Schlöndorff.
1978	75	Announcement that she is being considered for nomination to the Académie Française; Grace Frick's illness intensifies suggesting that the end is near; Jerry Wilson's first visit to Mount Desert in May with French TV crew; Yourcenar publishes her essay 'In the Manner of Dürer'; starts working on *Mishima*.
1979	76	Death of Grace Frick on 18 November; publication of *The Crown and the Lyre*, further translations of ancient Greek poetry; debates from November forward about Yourcenar's suitability for election to the French Academy in Paris; Jerry Wilson moves into Petite Plaisance for Christmas.
1980	77	Travels to Florida and the Caribbean with Jerry; 6 March, elected to the French Academy; gathers ideas for her acceptance speech; publication of *With Open Eyes*, interviews with Matthieu Galey; working on *Mishima*; further travels with Jerry all year; leaves for Europe with him in November.
1981	78	22 January, received into the French Academy; publication of her inaugural speech at French Academy; travels to Morocco with Jerry and then visits James Baldwin on the French Riviera; publication of *Mishima: A Vision of the Void* and her third volume of memoirs, *Anna, Soror*; publication of *Fires* in English; honorary doctorate, Harvard University; new version of 'In the Manner of Greco'.

Year	History	Culture
1962	Cuban missile crisis. Pompidou becomes French premier.	Solzhenitsin, *One Day in the Life of Ivan Denisovich*.
1963	J F Kennedy assassinated.	
1964	War on Poverty bill in America.	Sartre declines Nobel Prize.
1965	America bombs North Vietnam.	
1966	America bombs Hanoi.	
1967	Protests in America against Vietnam War.	
1968	Martin Luther King and Robert Kennedy assassinated. Violent student unrest in Paris.	Natalie Barney dies in December in Paris.
1969	De Gaulle resigns. Vietnam peace talks begin.	Beckett wins Nobel Prize.
1970	US invades Cambodia. De Gaulle dies.	Mishima commits suicide on 25 Nov.
1971	US invades Laos. Britain votes to join EEC.	American writer Henry Miller dies.
1972	Nixon visits China and Soviet Union.	Francis Ford Coppola, *The Godfather*.
1973	Vietnam Peace Treaty signed in Paris.	Toni Morrison, *Sula*.
1974	Nixon resigns after impeachment hearings, Pompidou dies. Giscard d'Estaing becomes President.	Muriel Spark, *Abbess of Crewe*.
1975	Vietcong capture Saigon. Death of Franco.	Ted Hughes, *Cave Birds*.
1976	Viking I and II land on Mars.	Margaret Atwood, *Lady Oracle*.
1977	President Carter pardons war draft evaders. First general election in Spain for 40 years. Steve Biko dies.	Susan Sontag, *On Photography* and *Illness as Metaphor*.
1978	Pope Paul VI and John Paul I both die; election of John Paul II. Nobel Peace Prize to Menachem Begin and Anwar Sadat.	Francesco Clemente, *Under the Hat*.
1979	James Jones mass cult suicide in Guyana. Iranian Hostage crisis.	Woody Allen, *Manhattan*. French writer Romain Gary dies.
1980	Eruption of Mount St Helens.	Alain Resnais, *My American Uncle*.
1981	First case of AIDS reported in California. First flight of the Space Shuttle.	Salman Rushdie, *Midnight's Children*. Milton Friedman, *Monetary Trends of the United States and the United Kingdom*.

Year	Age	Life
1982	79	Travels to Venice, Egypt, Kenya, India, Hawaii and Japan with Jerry Wilson; publication of *Like the Water that Flows*; publication in English of *A Coin in Nine Hands*; elected to the American Academy of Arts and Letters; *Prose Works* published in Bibliothèque de La Pléiade series.
1983	80	Travels with Jerry in Thailand, Greece, Kenya; publication of *That Mighty Sculptor, Time*; translates James Baldwin's play *The Amen Corner*; receives the Erasmus Prize; traffic accident in Kenya.
1984	81	Winter in Kenya recovering with Jerry; *Blues et Gospels* appears; *Alexis* published in English translated by Walter Kaiser; further travels with Jerry who makes a film about Mount Desert; travels interrupted by Jerry's illness; Jerry diagnosed as having AIDS; Kayaloff dies.
1985	82	Publication in English of *Oriental Tales*; Jerry Wilson seeking medical treatment in USA and Europe; Jerry leaves Maine and Yourcenar
1986	83	Jerry Wilson dies in Paris on 8 February 1986; publication of *The Dark Brain of Piranesi* and Alberto Manguel's Translation of *Mishima: A Vision of the Void* in English. Peter Conrad makes a documentary in which her life figures; she travels to Europe in November and remains in Paris all through the winter.
1987	84	In Morocco in March; returns to Petite Plaisance in May; lectures at Harvard University in October; final illness in November; hospitalized in Bar Harbor Hospital; dies on 17 December.
1988		Funeral service on Mount Desert Island on 16 January; very few French attendees.
1989		*What? Eternity*, the third volume of her memoirs, although unfinished, is posthumously published.
1990		
1991		*Dear Departed* appears in English; Josyanne Savigneau's official biography is published in French and English.
1995		*How Many Years* appears in English.
2003		Centenary of Yourcenar's birth.

Year	History	Culture
1982	Israel invades the Lebanon.	Ridley Scott, *Bladerunner*. Alice Munro, *The Moons of Jupiter*. The death of Carl Orff.
1983	Benigno Aquino assassinated.	J M Coetzee, *Life and Times of Michael K*.
1984	Introduction of the first Macintosh.	
1985	Rock Hudson comes out as a homosexual.	
1986	Arms control talks between the USA and the USSR begin in Reykjavik, Iceland.	
1987	Alan Greenspan becomes Chairman of the US Federal Reserve Bank.	Bertolucci, *The Last Emperor*. Death of Andy Warhol

Works by Marguerite Yourcenar

The list below is presented in nine sections, for the most part chronologically arranged except in those sub-sections where alphabetical arrangement is more convenient. Yourcenar's writings pose a daunting challenge for her biographers because she published her works in so many different versions and under such different titles. The reader is invited to consult the Chronology together with this list. Publishers are provided to show how Yourcenar circulated her works among publishing houses, revised her works and commented on them. Many of these works were reprinted in 1991 in *Oeuvres Romanesques*, the volume of Yourcenar's life and works she herself compiled in the Bibliothèque de la Pléiade (first published 1982). The list does not include Yourcenar's dozens of articles or the dates of the reprints of all her works, of which there were many during and after her lifetime.

1. PROSE FICTION

Alexis ou le traité du vain combat [Alexis or The Treatise on Vain Combat] (Paris, Au Sans Pareil: 1929); with preface added (Paris, Plon: 1952); revised edition (Paris, Plon: 1965); copyright holder (Paris, Gallimard: 1971)

La Nouvelle Eurydice [The New Eurydice] (Paris, Grasset: 1931)

La Mort conduit l'Attelage [Death Drives the Cart] (Paris, Grasset: 1934) Contains her stories 'In the Manner of' Rembrandt, El Greco and Dürer, reworked many times over many years

Denier du rêve [A Coin in Nine Hands] (Paris, Grasset: 1934); revised, enlarged, and with preface added (Paris, Plon: 1959); copyright holder (Paris, Gallimard: 1971)

Nouvelles orientales [Oriental Tales] (Paris, Gallimard: 1938); revised with preface added (1963); enlarged, definitive edition (1978)

Le Coup de grâce (Paris, Gallimard: 1939); with preface added (1966)

Mémoires d'Hadrien [Memoirs of Hadrian] (Paris, Plon: 1951); with

'Carnets de notes des *Mémoires d'Hadrien*' (Paris, Plon: 1958); copyright holder (Gallimard: 1971 and 1974).
L'Oeuvre au noir [The Abyss], (Paris, Gallimard: 1968); reprinted (1982), (1988)
Comme l'eau qui coule [Like the Water that Flows], (Paris, Gallimard: 1982); contains 'Un homme obscur', 'Un belle matinee'.
Oeuvres romanesques [Prose Works] (Paris, Gallimard: 1982)
Le Cheval noir à tete blanche [The Black Horse with the White Head] (Paris, Gallimard: 1985)
La Voix des choses [The Voice of Things] (Paris, Gallimard: 1987)
En pélerin en étranger [A Pilgrim and a Stranger] (Paris, Gallimard: 1989)
Conte blue, Le premier soir, Maléfice [A Tale of a Tub: The first night, evil spell] (Paris, Gallimard: 1993)

2. NONFICTION PROSE

Pindare (Paris, Grasset: 1932)
Les Songes et les sorts [Dreams and Destinies] (Paris, Grasset: 1938)
L'Ecrivain devant l'Histoire [The Writer in the Face of History] (Paris, Centre national de documentation pédagogique: 1954)
Sous bénéfice d'inventaire [The Dark Brain of Piranesi] (Paris, Gallimard: 1962); enlarged and definitive edition (1978)
Le Labyrinthe du Monde [The Labyrinth of the World], I: *Souvenirs pieux* [Dear Departed] (Paris, Gallimard: 1974)
Le Labyrinthe du Monde, II, *Archives du Nord* [How Many Years] (Paris, Gallimard: 1977)
Anna, soror (Paris, Gallimard: 1981)
Mishima ou la vision du Vide [Mishima: A Vision of the Void] (Paris, Gallimard: 1981)
Discours de réception de l'Académie Française [Acceptance Speech into the French Academy] (Paris, Gallimard: 1981)
Le Temps, ce grand sculpteur [That Mighty Sculptor, Time] (Paris, Gallimard: 1983): collection of essays published in various journals
Blues et Gospels (Paris, Gallimard: 1984)
Le Labyrinthe du Monde [The Labyrinth of the World], III, *Quoi? L'Eternité* [What? Eternity] (Paris, Gallimard: 1988)

Le Tour de la prison [This, Our Prison] (Paris, la Pléiade: 1991): essays and memoirs

3. THEATRE

Electre ou la chute des masques [Electra or the Fall of the Masks] (Paris, Plon: 1954)
Le mystère d'Alceste and *Qui n'a pas son Minotaure?* [To Each his Minotaur] (Paris, Plon: 1963)
Théâtre, two volumes (Paris, Gallimard: 1971)

4. POETRY

Le jardin des chimères [The Garden of Illusions] (Paris, Perrin: 1921)
Les Dieux ne sont pas morts [The Gods are not Dead] (Paris, Chiberre: 1922)
Feux [Fires] (Paris, Grasset: 1936); with a different preface (Paris, Plon: 1957); revised (Paris, Plon: 1968); copyright holder (Paris, Gallimard: 1974)
Les Charités d'Alcippe et autres poèmes [The Alms of Alcippus] (Liege, La Flute enchanté: 1956)

5. TRANSLATIONS INTO FRENCH

Woolf, Virginia, *Les Vagues* [The Waves] (Paris, Stock: 1937)
James, Henry, *Ce que savait Maisie* [What Maisie Knew] (Paris, Laffont: 1947)
Cavafy, Constantine, *Poèmes*, in collaboration with Constantine Dimaras (Paris, Gallimard: 1958)
Fleuve profonde, sombre rivière [Deep River, Dark River] (Paris, Gallimard: 1964): African-American spirituals
Flexner, Hortense, *Poèmes* (Paris, Gallimard: 1969)
Baldwin, James, *Le Coin des 'Amen'* [The Amen Corner] (Paris, Gallimard: 1983)
La Couronne et la lyre [The Crown and the Lyre] (Paris, Gallimard: 1979)
Mishima, Yukio, *Cinq Nô modernes de Yukio Mishima* [Five Modern Noh Plays] in collaboration with Jun Shiragi (Paris, Gallimard: 1984)
Blues et gospels (Paris, Gallimard: 1984)

6. INTERVIEWS

A. BOOKS

Rosbo, Patrick de, *Entretiens radiophoniques avec Marguerite Yourcenar* (Paris, Mercure de France: 1972)

Wakeman, John (ed) *World Authors 1950–1970* (New York, H W Wilson: 1975): includes an 'Autobiographical Sketch' of Yourcenar

Les Yeux ouverts: Entretiens avec Matthieu Galey [With Open Eyes] (Paris, Le Centurion: 1980)

B. SELECTED NEWSPAPERS AND PERIODICALS

Les Nouvelles littéraires, 22 May 1952, p 6
Le Figaro littéraire, 3 October 1959, p 8
'Le Questionnaire Proust', *Livres de France*, May 1964, pp 11–13
Les Nouvelles littéraires, 27 June 1968, p 3
Les Lettres françaises, 27 November 1968, p 20
Le Figaro littéraire, 2 December 1968, pp 20–21
Le Nouvel Observateur, 2 December 1968, pp 44–45
Le Figaro littéraire, 18 June 1971, p 28
Réalités, October 1974, pp 70–76
Le Figaro, 26 November 1977, p 19
US News and World Report, 28 July 1980, p 61

C. RADIO

Chancel, Jacques, Radioscopie, France Inter/Radio France, 11–15 June 1979.

D. TELEVISION

Documentary of the life of Marguerite Yourcenar, USA, 1992

7. EDITORIALS, PUBLISHED LETTERS, INTRODUCTIONS, PREFACES

'Mythologie', January 1944, *Lettres françaises*, number 11, pp 141–46
'Letter to Etienne Coche de la Ferté', September 1963, in 'Madame Yourcenar et les scrupules du poète.' *Cahiers des Saisons* 38 (1964): p 302

'Letter', *Le Monde*, 2–3 March 1969, p 12

'Letter to Alain Bosquet', 6 June 1969, in *Marginales* 24 (1969) pp 85–86.

'Letters to Léonie Siret', 20 July 1969 and 17 January 1971, in *La Nouvelle Revue française*, 1 April 1980, pp 181–91

'Une Civilisation à cloisons étanches', *Le Figaro*, 16 February 1972, p 1 Editorial. Reprinted in *Le Temps, ce grand sculpteur*, pp 191–95, Paris: Gallimard, 1983

'Letter to Yvon Bernier', 4 January 1978, in 'Itineraire d'une oeuvre', *Etudes littéraires*, 12 (1979), p 8

Introduction to Roger Caillois, *The Writing of the Stones* (Charlottesville, Virginia: 1985), pp 1–5

8. COLLECTIONS OF LETTERS

Sarde, Michèle, et al, *Marguerite Yourcenar: Lettres à ses amis et quelques autres* (Paris: 1995). This edition of Yourcenar's letters is vital for identifying her correspondents and reconstructing her library at Petite Plaisance, Mount Desert Island, Maine

9. TRANSLATIONS OF SELECTED WORKS INTO ENGLISH

'The Man Who Loved the Nereids', in *National and English Review* (Dec 1937) pp 783–88. Translated by David Freeman

'The Milk of Death', in *National and English Review* (Sept 1939) pp 359–366. Translated by David Freeman

Memoirs of Hadrian, translated by Grace Frick in collaboration with the author (New York, Farrar, Straus & Giroux: 1954); with 'Reflections on the Composition of the *Memoirs of Hadrian*' (New York, Farrar, Straus & Giroux: 1963)

Coup de Grace, translated by Grace Frick in collaboration with the author (New York, Farrar, Straus & Giroux: 1957)

The Abyss, translated by Grace Frick in collaboration with the author (New York, Farrar, Straus & Giroux: 1976)

Fires, translated by Dori Katz in collaboration with the author (New York, Farrar, Straus & Giroux: 1981)

The Alms of Alcippus, translated by Edith R Farrell (New York, Targ Editions: 1982)

A Coin in Nine Hands, translated by Dori Katz in collaboration with the author (New York, Farrar, Straus & Giroux: 1982)

Plays, translated by Dori Katz in collaboration with the author (New York, Performing Arts Journal Publications: 1984)

With Open Eyes, translated by Arthur Goldhammer (Boston, Beacon Press: 1984)

The Dark Brain of Piranesi and Other Essays, translated by Richard Howard in collaboration with the author (New York, Farrar, Straus & Giroux: 1984): contains 'Humanism and Occultism in Thomas Mann', translated by Grace Frick in collaboration with the author

Alexis, translated by Walter Kaiser in collaboration with the author (New York, Farrar, Straus and Giroux: 1984)

Oriental Tales, translated by Alberto Manguel in collaboration with the author (New York, Farrar, Straus and Giroux: 1985)

Mishima: A Vision of the Void, translated by Alberto Manguel in collaboration with the author (New York, Farrar, Straus & Giroux: 1986)

Dear Departed: a memoir, translated by Maria Louise Ascher (New York, Farrar, Straus & Giroux: 1991)

How Many Years, translated by Maria Louise Ascher (New York: 1995)

Dreams and Destinies, translated by Donald Flanell Friedman (New York, St Martin's Press: 1999)

Further Reading

The main collection of primary material for any study of Yourcenar's biography is the Harvard University Yourcenar Archive in the Houghton Library, Cambridge, Massachusetts, USA. Since Yourcenar's death in 1987 a vast industry devoted to commentary on her work has arisen, especially in the Belgian universities and those of northern France, producing important articles, books, study centres and colloquia. There are over 100 websites devoted to the compilation of information about her life and works.

Benstock, Shari, *Women on the Left Bank: 1900–1940* (London: 1986)
Bentley, Eric, 'We are in History: An Interview' in G Stambolian, *Homosexualities and French Literature* (Ithaca, NY: 1979) pp 122–40
Birley, A R, *Hadrian: the restless emperor* (London: 1997)
Blot, Jean, *Marguerite Yourcenar* (Paris: 1971). Second edition: 1980
Castle, Terry, *The Apparitional Lesbian: Female Homosexuality and Modern Culture* (New York: 1993)
Doan, Laura L, *Fashioning Sapphism: the Origins of a Modern English Lesbian Culture* (New York: 2001)
Dodds, E R, *The Greeks and the Irrational* (Berkeley, CA: 1951)
Farrell, C F, and E R Farrell, *Marguerite Yourcenar in Counterpoint* (Lanham, MD: 1983)
Flanner, J, *Paris was yesterday, 1925–1939* (London: 1973)
Fryer, Jonathan, *Christopher Isherwood: A Biography* (New York: 1977)
Goslar, Michelle, *Le visage secret de Marguerite Yourcenar* (Tournai: 2001)
Heilbut, Anthony, *Thomas Mann: Eros and Literature* (New York: 1995)
Isherwood, Christopher, *Goodbye to Berlin* (London: 1939)
Jung, Carl and K Kerényi, *Psychology and Alchemy* (London: 1992) [reprint of 1956 and 1974]
Kahn, Madeleine, *Narrative Transvestism* (Ithaca, NY: 1991)

Kaiser, Walter, 'Marguerite Yourcenar' in *Essays on Greatness* (Cambridge, MA: 1983)

Kemp, Peter, 'Intensely Individual' in the *Times Literary Supplement* (21 February 1986) p 192

Kerényi, K, *Eleusis: Archetypal Image of Mother and Daughter* (London: 1967)

Poignault, Rémy (ed), *Bulletin de la Société Internationale d'Etudes Yourcenariennes* volumes 1 to 23 (1987–2002)

Renault, Mary, 'History in Fiction' in the *Times Literary Supplement* (1973), p 315

———, 'Souvenirs pieux' in the *Times Literary Supplement* (1974), p 894

Saint, Nigel, *Marguerite Yourcenar: Reading the Visual* (Oxford: 2000)

Sarde, Michèle, *Vous, Marguerite Yourcenar* (Paris: 1995)

Savigneau, Josyanne, *Marguerite Yourcenar: Inventing a Life*, trans by Joan E Howard (New York: 1991): the authoritative biography

Shurr, Georgia, *Marguerite Yourcenar, A Reader's Guide* (Fairlawn, NJ: 1987)

Syme, Ronald, *Roman Papers: Six Volumes* (Oxford: 1991): volume 6 reprints Syme's critique of *Memoirs of Hadrian*.

Wachman, Gay, *Lesbian Empire: radical crosswriting in the Twenties* (New Brunswick, NJ: 2001)

Weiss, Andrea, *Paris Was a Woman: Portraits from the Left Bank* (London: 1995)

White, Edmund, *The Burning Library: Writings on Art, Politics and Sexuality 1969–1993* (London: 1994) pp 350–54: originally appeared as a review of Josyanne Savigneau's biography

Picture Sources

The author and publishers wish to express their thanks to the following sources of illustrative material and/or permission to reproduce it. They will make proper acknowledgements in future editions in the event that any omissions have occurred.

AKG London: pp. 3, Corbis: pp. 53, 70, 75, 101, 115, The Lebrecht Picture Library/Rue des Archives: pp. iii, v, 7, 10, 23, 48, Topham Picturepoint: pp. 37, 44, 61, 64, 77, 90, 108, 112,

A Note on the Author

George Rousseau is a member of the Faculty of Modern history at the University of Oxford. He has written many books and articles about the influence of cultural history on individual life, most recently *Gout: The Patrician malady* (1999) with the late Roy Porter.

Index

Académie Française, 1, 4, 81, 106, 115, 121–2; history, 111
Adamites, 88
Aegean Sea, 41
African-American spirituals, 17, 52, 112–13
Agdistis, 92
AIDS, 11, 113, 121–2
Albania, 6
Alexander the Great, 123
Alexis, 2, 4, 16, 31–3, 35, 117, 126
Algeria, 38
Alps, 39, 44, 48, 59
Alto Adige, 39
ambition, 28
America, 17, 49–53, 56–9, 77, 94–6, 100, 103, 106, 110, 119, 127; academia, 103; AIDS in, 113; feminists, 98; Civil Rights Movement, 96; Gay Liberation, 96, 121; lesbian movement, 121; Mishima visits, 108; Negro cause, 123; the South, 111, 112–13
Amsterdam, 111
Ananke, 103, 113
ancient world, 1, 3, 26–7, 34, 68, 72
Antinopolis, 67, 74
Antinous, 2, 17–19, 55, 57, 61–2, 67–70, 73–6, 90, 120, 123; Mondragone, 27
Aristophanes, 25
Arkansas, 107
Ascher, Maria Louise, 15
Athens, 43–4
Aubrion, Michel, 97
Auden, W H, 50, 57, 66–7
Austen, Jane, 71
Austria, 39, 46

Bach, Johann Sebastian, 5
Baldwin, James, 112
Balzac, Honoré de, 25
Bar Harbor Hospital, 100, 116
Barnes, Julian, quoted, 1, 18
Barney, Natalie, 12–13, 120
Barrès, Michel, 25
Baubo, 92, 93
Baudelaire, Charles, 64
Beach, Sylvia, 24
Beckmann, Max, 58
Belgian Academy, 99
Bentley, Eric, 122–3
Berlin, 57
Blaes, J B, 93
Bordeaux, 48, 51
Borges, Jorge Luis, 36, 114
Bosch, Hieronymus, 93, 105
Boulez, Pierre, 81
Breughel, Pieter, 5, 27, 105; *The Temptation of St Anthony*, 62
Bruges, 84–7, 100, 111
Bruno, Giordano, 16, 89

Brussels, 8, 100, 110
Bryher, Winifred, 119
Buddha, 83
Buddhism, 25, 118
Byron, Lord, 63; *Don Juan*, 69

Campanella, Tommaso, 16, 85, 89
Camus, Albert, 81
Caravaggio, 52
Castle, Terry, 125
Catherine de Medici, 82, 86, 92
Catholicism, 16, 26
Cavafy, Constantine, 4, 18, 43–4, 46, 49–50, 79, 82; biography, 44
Cesalpino, 89
Charles V, Emperor, 83
Charleston, 50
Chateaubriand, 25
Chekhov, Anton, 3
Chenonceaux, 82
Chirac, Jacques, 90
Christianity, 16, 64–7, 93, 118
Church of Rome, 85
Cicero, 63
Cocteau, Jean, 3, 41, 81, 109
Colette, 120
Columbia University, 48, 49
Comenius, 104, 105
Connecticut, 51
Corneille, Pierre, 25, 111

INDEX   149

Crayencour, Berthe de, 21
Crayencour, Christine de, *see* Hoevelt, Christine
Crayencour, Fernande de, 8; death, 5, 21; possible liaison with Jeanne de Vietinghoff, 32
Crayencour, Michel de Cleenewerck de, 10, 24–7, 29, 33, 37, 40, 116; relationship with Marguerite, 2, 8, 21–2, 36, 120; death, 8, 36, 46, 55, 79; and Fernande's death, 21; third marriage, 29–30; affair with Jeanne de Vietinghoff, 32; library, 93; translation of Comenius, 104; religion, 118
Crayencour, Michel de, 21
Crayencour, Noémi de, 21
Crayencour family, 100, 104, 113
cross-gendered writing, 19, 98, 119–20
cummings, e e, 24
Cyprian the sodomite, 18

De Gaulle, General, 50
de Sévigné, Madame, 71
death, 16–17, 20, 74–5, 94, 109
Deffand, Madame du, 71
des Genettes, Madame Roger (La Sylphide), 63
Descartes, René, 83
despair, 25
Diane de Poitiers, 82
Dickens, Charles, 30
Dimaras, Constantine, 43–4
Dodds, E R, *The Greeks and the Irrational*, 66

Dolet, Étienne, 89
Dos Passos, John, 24
Dostoevsky, Fedor, 17, 25
Dumay, Maurice, 107
Dürer, Albrecht, 4, 5–6, 83, 93, 106–7; *Melancholia*, 63, 83; *Traumgesicht*, 83, 106
Durrell, Lawrence, 125
Dutch, 24, 88

Egypt, 68, 111
El Greco, 107
Eleusis, 80, 92, 93
Eliade, Mircea, 93–4; *The Forge and the Crucible*, 94
Eliot, George, 71
Embiricos, André, 41, 43
Empedocles, 67, 102
England, 22, 33, 111
English, 6, 8, 15, 24, 25, 51, 56, 78, 96
Enlightenment, 4
Epictetus, 67
Epicureanism, 65
Erasmus, 89
erotic love, 19–20, 28, 35, 64, 67–70, 74, 80–1, 90, 109, 122–3
essays, 2, 4, 5, 103, 112
Euphrates, 67
Euripides, 4, 25, 34
Europe, 17, 36, 46, 50, 57, 60, 84, 87, 91, 99–100, 114–15; lesbian movement, 121; Nazi, 56, 58; Yourcenar's 'Diagnostic', 30

Farrar Straus, 14
Farrell, Edith R, 15
Fasquelle (publishers), 69
Faust, 85, 89, 94
feminist criticism, 4, 19, 98, 116, 119, 122, 124–5
Fitzgerald, F. Scott, 24
Flamel, Nicholas, 89
Flaubert, Gustave, 18, 25, 62–6; sexual ambivalence, 64; *Madame Bovary*, 34, 64
Flemish, 24, 88
Flexner, Hortense, 102
Flinker, Martin, 80, 81
Florence, 29, 68
Fraigneau, André, 30, 40–3, 45–6, 105; biography, 41
France, 2, 31, 48, 51, 59, 60, 98, 111, 119; Flemish, 104; Yourcenar's reputation, 96, 116
Freeman, David, 15
French, 15, 17, 24, 25, 52, 56, 79, 95, 107, 110, 114
Freud, Sigmund, 73, 110
Frick, Grace, 12–13, 45–6, 48, 49–57, 59–60, 76, 79–80, 97, 111–13, 116; relationship with Yourcenar, 8–10, 14, 20, 54, 57, 78, 99–101, 106, 118; death, 9, 11, 15, 20, 83, 106, 110, 113; Yourcenar's translator, 9, 15, 78, 100, 105–6, 110; money, 9, 10, 12; illness, 60, 100–2, 105, 107, 109–10; love of children, 99; good listener, 114; memory of, 115

Galey, Matthieu, 41, 75, 121
Gallimard (publishers), 14, 45, 60, 95, 99, 102, 108, 112–13
Galsworthy, John, 30
gender, 19, 47, 95–6, 111,

118–19, 123–4
Genet, Jean, 81
German, 8, 24, 76–7
Germany, 48
Gide, André, 3, 18, 31, 33, 37, 46, 119, 124; biography, 38; influence on Yourcenar, 25, 37–8, 46, 102; style, 38, 46; Yourcenar's essay, 103
Gnosticism, 64, 66
Goethe, Johann Wolfgang von, 25, 81, 89
Goldhammer, Arthur, 15
Goll, Claire, 76
Göteborg, 76
Grand Prix National des Lettres, 103, 105–6
Grand Prix of the Académie Française, 106
Grasset, Bernard, 14, 40
Grasset (publishers), 14, 38, 41, 45, 60
Greece, 6, 40–2, 44, 46, 49, 50, 79; ancient, 19, 93, 117, 119; religion, 38, 118
Greek, 8, 26, 30
Gubar, Susan, 122
Guyon, Madame, 45

Hadrian, Emperor, 2–4, 12, 16, 19, 27, 35, 55, 57–62, 66–70, 72–7, 80–1, 83–4, 90–3, 95–7, 116–21, 126; biography, 67; British Museum bronze, 22, 61; cult of death, 74–5; melancholy, 67–8, 73–4; suicide, 73; travels, 18, 39; Yourcenar's identification with, 58, 62, 97, 103, 107, 109, 123, 127

Hall, Radclyffe, 4, 119; *The Well of Loneliness*, 40
Hartford, 51–2, 54, 56, 105, 113
Harvard University, 4, 17, 53, 114, 116
Hausrath, Adolf, *Antinous*, 68
Heilbut, Anthony, 77
Hellenism, 42, 44
Hemingway, Ernest, 24
Henri II, 82, 92
Henri III, 31
hermeticism, 16
Herodotus, 34
historical novel, 2
Hitler, Adolf, 51
Hoevelt, Christine, 27, 29–30, 51, 82
Homage from France to Thomas Mann, 81
homosexuality, 2, 33, 38, 42–3, 57, 74, 83, 109, 118–19, 121–2, 126; *see also* same-sex love
Howard, Richard, 15, 82
Hugo, Victor, 25
Huysmans, J K, 25

Ibsen, Henrik, 25
Icarus, 27
incest, 28, 29, 42
India, 27, 111
Innsbruck, 39
Inquisition, 85–7, 126
Isherwood, Christopher, 50, 57, 99; quoted, 49
Italian, 8, 24
Italy, 6, 28, 37, 39, 60

Jaloux, Edmond, 35; review of *Alexis*, 34
James, Henry, 4; *What Maisie Knew*, 54
Janina, 50
Japan, 108, 109, 111
Jensen, Wilhelm, *Gradiva*, 42, 110
Joyce, James, 3, 6; *Ulysses*, 24
Jung, Carl Gustav, 16, 93, 94

Kaiser, Walter, 15, 114
Kansas City, 8
Kassner, Rudolph, 40
Katz, Dori, 15
Kayaloff, Jacques, 51–2, 54
Kemp, Peter, 117
Kennedy, Robert, 96
Kenya, 111
Kerényi, Karl, 16, 92, 93, 94
King, Martin Luther, 96
Kyriakos, Lucy, 43–6, 50

La Bruyère, Jean de, 25
labyrinth, 42, 104–5
Lady Macbeth, 121
Larbaud, Valéry, 81
Latin, 8, 26
Lausanne, 37, 55
Le Milieu du Siècle, 54
Leonardo da Vinci, 89
Les Nouvelles Littéraires, 34
lesbians, 40, 91, 119–22, 125; writers, 4, 19, 124–5
Librarie Plon (publishers), 14, 59–60, 95, 99, 102
literature, 26, 117; French, 26, 64; gay, 123–4; Oriental, 25, 30, 109
London, 22, 24, 44
Louvre, 24, 27
Low Countries, 28, 84
Lowell, Robert, 12
Lucretius, 58, 63–5, 70; *De rerum natura*, 65

INDEX 151

Maeterlinck, Maurice, 25
Magic Flute, The, 81
Maine, 5, 9, 13–14, 17–18, 46, 51–2, 56, 58, 76, 82, 94, 116; universities, 103
Malraux, André, 81
Manguel, Alberto, 15
Mann, Thomas, 3, 4, 12, 18, 77, 102, 119, 125; writes to Yourcenar, 76–7; Yourcenar's essay, 79–81, 124; *Buddenbrooks*, 77, 80
Marcus Aurelius, 3, 60, 63, 66–8, 70
Margaret of Austria, 91
Marlowe, Christopher, 89
Mary Queen of Scots, 121
Medea, 121
Mediterranean Sea, 17, 41, 84
melancholy, 63–4, 73–4
mentalities, 83
Merezhkovsky, Dmitri Sergeyevich, 25
Mesures, 49
Michelangelo, 4
Middle Ages, 8, 29
Milan, 29
Miller, Henry, 24
Mishima, Yukio, 2, 12, 109, 125; biography, 108
misogyny, 4, 93
Modernism, 3, 34, 119, 124
Monicah (nurse), 115
Mont Noir, 8, 21, 22, 110
Monte Carlo, 24, 30
Montherlant, Henri, 3
Morand, Paul, 33
Morocco, 111
Mount Desert Island, 9–11, 52–6, 60, 79, 99, 102, 109, 121

Mussolini, Benito, 39
myths, 56–7; Greek, 26, 42, 43

Naples, 28, 29
Nathanaël, 4, 107, 117
Nazis, 50, 58
New Haven, 55, 66
New York, 48, 50, 52, 55, 66, 113
Nietzsche, Friedrich, 25
Nile, River, 18
Noh plays, 25, 110
novella, 2

occult, 6, 27, 61, 65–6, 74, 80–1, 84, 97, 126–7
Omar Khayyám, 27

painting, 5–6, 23, 29, 83, 105
Paracelsus, 16, 89
Paré, Ambroise, 89
Paris, 8, 12, 14, 22–6, 28, 30, 40–1, 51, 56, 113–15, 118; anti-Semitism, 39; bookshops, 24, 66; Hôtel Wagram, 40, 45; liberation, 54; literary and publishing world, 59–60, 79–80, 95, 100, 110–11, 122; newspapers, 106; occupation, 50; student unrest, 95, 96; theatres, 23
Parker, Alice, 51
Petite Plaisance, 53, 56, 101, 107, 113, 115
Peyrefitte, Roger, 81
Phèdre, 121
philosophy, 22, 25, 26, 73, 93
Picasso, Pablo, 81

Pilgrim's Progress (Bunyan), 105
Pindar, 4, 26, 30, 34, 37–9, 40–1
Piranesi, Giambattista, 4, 5, 12
Pirmez, Octave and Rémo, 5, 18, 104
Po Valley, 39
Pound, Ezra, 24
Poupet, Georges, 14, 59
Prix Femina Vacaresco, 60
Proust, Marcel, 3, 6, 19

Racine, Jean, 23, 25, 111
Ratisbon, 39
récit, 38, 46
Reformation, 19, 84–5, 92–3
Reisiger, Hans, 76
Rembrandt, 5–6, 107; *Polish Rider*, 5
Renaissance, 1, 3, 26–7, 68, 79, 83, 87–9, 92–3, 104; artists, 63, 107; occultism, 27
Renault, Mary, 119, 123
Reni, Guido, 109
Rilke, Rainer Maria, 33, 34
Rimini, 29
Rolland, Romain, 25
Romains, Jules, 81
Roman Empire, 18, 67, 72, 90
Romaniticism, 3, 26, 119
Rome, 29, 82; ancient, 19, 68, 84, 90, 117, 119; Fascist, 39
Ruysdael, Jacob van, 4, 5

Sade, Marquis de, 109
Saint Paul-de-Vence, 112
Saint-Jans-Cappel, 21

same-sex love, 2, 19, 76, 122–4, 127
Sand, Georges, 71
Santa Fe, 55
Sappho, 121
Sarah Lawrence College, 12, 52–3, 55
Sartre, Jean-Paul, 81, 96
Savigneau, Josyanne, 42, 49, 99, 113
Scheveningen, 32
Schlumberger, Jean, 80, 81
Schopenhauer, Arthur, 25
Seneca, 67
Servetus, Michael, 87, 89
Shakespeare, William, 22, 25
short story, 2
Smith College, 103
sodomy, 86, 87, 91
Sophocles, 34
Spain, 60, 100
Spanish, 8
Stambolian, Georges, 122
Stein, Gertrude, 3, 6, 24, 56
Sterne, Laurence, 114
Stoicism, 16, 65, 66–7, 70, 93
Straus, Roger, 14
Styron, William, 125
Sureau, François, 125
Sutton Island, 102
Switzerland, 39, 55
Syme, Sir Ronald, 72

Tagore, Rabindranath, 27
Tate no Kai (Shield Society), 108
Teresa of Avila, 45
Thatcher, Margaret, 111
Thucydides, 34
Times Literary Supplement, 112
Toklas, Alice, 6

Tolstoy, Leo, 3, 17; 'Kreutzer Sonata', 25
Trajan, Emperor, 3, 61, 67
Treaty of Cambrai, 91

Valéry, Paul, 31
Var, 77, 80
Venice, 29, 111
Verona, 29
Vesalius, 89
Vienna, 40
Vietinghoff, Conrad de, 32
Vietinghoff, Egon de, 32
Vietinghoff, Jeanne de, 32
Vietnam, 96
Villa Adriana, 62, 67, 68
Virgil, *Aeneid*, 28

Wachman, Gay, 119
Warner, Sylvia Townsend, 4, 119
Westchester County, 53–4
Wharton, Edith, 4
Wilde, Oscar, 33–4, 38; biography, 33; *De Profundis*, 19, 33, 38
Wilson, Jerry, 10–11, 17, 107, 110–12, 118, 120–1; death, 11, 114; AIDS, 11, 113; memory of, 115; *Blues and Gospels*, 112
wine, 15
With Open Eyes, 22, 25, 27, 41, 75, 84, 121
women, 2, 4–6, 19, 29, 71–2, 119–22, 125; rights, 122
Woolf, Virginia, 3, 4, 9, 44–5, 103, 119; *The Waves*, 44
World War One, 24, 26, 46, 118
World War Two, 2

Yourcenar, Marguerite (Marguerite Antoinette Jeanne Marie Ghislaine de Crayencour): historical imagination, 1, 2, 72–3, 117; pessimism, 1–2, 16, 25, 39, 58; father's influence, 2, 8, 21–2, 36, 120; style, 2, 7, 13, 15, 16, 33, 34, 95, 125; reputation, 3–4, 96, 116; autobiographical works, 4, 26, 43, 104, 112; visual sense, 5–6, 23; lack of innovation, 4–6; classicism, 6–7, 15, 19–20, 34, 58, 66, 81; sexuality, 6, 41, 50, 56, 118–21, 127; seductions, 6, 8, 11, 18, 20, 118; self-confidence, 7; secretiveness, 7, 71–2, 119, 126–7; appearance, 8, 43; birth, 8; Yourcenar name, 8, 27, 29; childhood, 8, 21; education, 8, 23–7, 34; travel, 8–11, 13, 17–20, 29, 39, 84, 94, 101, 103, 110–12, 115, 127; relationship with Grace Frick, 8–10, 14, 20, 54, 57, 78, 99–101, 106, 118; money, 9, 10, 12–13, 14, 24, 36, 48, 50–1, 53, 57, 127; health, 9, 100, 114, 116, 127; hypochondria, 9, 12, 52, 116; moods, 9; relationship with Jerry Wilson, 10–11, 107, 110, 112, 118, 120–1; death, 12, 17, 116; geographical isolation,

12–13; male friends, 13; hedonism, 13, 16; correspondence, 13, 82, 101–2, 121, 126; relations with publishers, 13–14, 59–60, 79, 82, 95, 99, 102, 106; self-belief, 14; revision and recasting, 15–16, 29, 79, 107, 124; religion, 16, 26, 118; Greek and Italian period, 17; languages, 24, 26; reading, 25, 64, 93; jealousy, 29; *flâneuse*, 36; period of dissipation, 40; relationship with André Fraigneau, 41, 42–3, 45–6, 105; Pléiade biography, 41, 71, 125; relationship with Lucy Kyriakos, 43–6, 50; meets Virginia Woolf, 44–5, 103; meets Grace Frick and travels to New York, 45, 48, 49; dreams, 45; dark years, 49, 105; American citizenship, 54, 59, 110; awards and honours, 60, 99–100, 103, 105–6; 'Carnets', 83; pride, 94, 95, 122, 124; identification with Hadrian and Zeno, 58, 62, 97–8, 103, 107, 109, 123, 127; unease with children, 99; riding, 102–3; lecture tours, 103; election to Académie Française, 106, 110–11, 121–2; meets James Baldwin, 112; conversation, 114; meets Borges, 114; reception after death, 116; maturity of vision, 117; Sapphic theory, 121

WORKS: *The Abyss*, 4, 5, 15–16, 18, 27, 28, 31, 39–40, 56, 79, 82–97, 99–100, 105–6, 109, 113; *Alexis*, 15, 19, 31–4, 36–8, 42, 46, 69, 71, 102–3, 126; *The Alms of Alcippus*, 80, 82; *Anna Soror*, 28; *Blues and Gospels*, 112; *A Coin in Nine Hands*, 15, 39, 79, 82, 102; *Coup de Grâce*, 46–7; *The Crown and the Lyre*, 108; *The Dark Brain of Piranesi*, 5, 82; *Dear Departed*, 5, 15, 18, 21, 29, 104; *Death Drives the Cart*, 42; *Deep River, Dark River*, 113; *Dreams and Destinies*, 45; *Electra*, 54, 76, 79–82; *Fires*, 43, 71; *The Garden of Illusions*, 27; *The Gods are not Dead*, 27; *How Many Years*, 22, 30, 104; 'In the Manner of Dürer', 28, 42, 79; 'In the Manner of El Greco', 28, 42; 'In the Manner of Rembrandt', 28, 42; *The Labyrinth of the World*, 104, 106, 113, 116; *Like the Water that Flows*, 28; *Memoirs of Hadrian*, 1, 4, 15, 17, 24, 27, 39, 49, 53, 55, 59–78, 79–84, 90, 92, 95, 97, 122, 125; *Mishima: A Vision of the Void*, 15, 109; 'An Obscure Man', 28, 107, 109; *Oriental Tales*, 45, 113; *Pindar*, 30; 'Reflections on the Composition of *Memoirs of Hadrian*', 28, 71, 79; *That Mighty Sculptor, Time*, 112; *To Each his Minotaur*, 105; *What? Eternity*, 101, 104

Zeno, 2–4, 12, 16, 18, 39–40, 79, 81, 83–97, 100, 117–18, 121, 126; suicide, 73, 89; Yourcenar's identification with, 97, 103, 107, 109